new testament

NIrV, The Books of the Bible for Kids: New Testament
Copyright © 2017 by Biblica
Illustrations © 2017 by Zondervan

The Holy Bible, *New International Reader's Version*®
Copyright © 1995, 1996, 1998, 2014 by Biblica, Inc.®
All rights reserved

Published by Zonderkidz
3900 *Sparks Dr. SE, Grand Rapids, Michigan 49546, U.S.A.*

www.zonderkidz.com

Library of Congress Catalog Card Number 2017941837

17 18 19 20 21 22 23 24 25 /DCI/ 20 19 18 17 16 15 14 13 12 11 10 9 8 7 6 5 4 3 2 1

You will be pleased to know that a portion of the purchase price of your new NIrV Bible has been provided to Biblica, Inc.® to help spread the gospel of Jesus Christ around the world!

Contents

introduction to the New Testament

The New Testament is a collection of books written many years ago. Together, they tell the story of Jesus and the very first people who followed him. The New Testament is also part of a much bigger collection known as "the Bible."

Long ago, the Bible tells us, God created the world. Everything he made was good. But creation turned its back on God. Suddenly, the whole world was held captive by sin and death.

So God set out to rescue us—to save us from sin and death and make things right. The story came to a climax two thousand years ago, when Jesus of Nazareth, the Son of God, came to earth.

As you read these stories and letters from the New Testament, you'll hear about how Jesus came to rescue us. You'll hear how his very first followers lived—and sometimes died—for him.

But don't just read these stories. You're invited to become part of the story. Because it's not over. God is still at work. And you have a part to play.

LUKE-ACTS, PART 1

introduction to Luke-Acts, part 1

The story you're about to read was written by a doctor named Luke. Luke wanted his friend Theophilus to know about Jesus, so he wrote a book. Two books, actually: the Gospel of Luke and the book of Acts.

In the first book, God keeps a promise he made to the people of Israel (who were called Jews) by sending Jesus, their long-awaited King.

But Jesus also invites non-Jewish people called Gentiles to follow him, because Jesus loves everyone. This was very good news, especially for Theophilus, who might have been a Gentile himself.

Luke worked hard to make sure he got his facts right. He wanted Theophilus to know he could bet his life on this story. So Luke used many reliable sources. Can you guess what some of them might've been?

Well, there were letters and speeches; songs and travel journals; notes from when people went to court; testimonies from eyewitnesses who knew Jesus; and more.

As you read, remember: this is not just any story. This is the true story of Jesus.

Many people have attempted to write about the things that have taken place among us. Reports of these things were handed down to us. There were people who saw these things for themselves from the beginning. They saw them and then passed the word on. With this in mind, I myself have carefully looked into everything from the beginning. So I also decided to write down an orderly report of exactly what happened. I am doing this for you, most excellent Theophilus. I want you to know that the things you have been taught are true.

⟨∽∞⟩

In the sixth month after Elizabeth had become pregnant, God sent the angel Gabriel to Nazareth, a town in Galilee. He was sent to a virgin. The girl was engaged to a man named Joseph. He came from the family line of David. The virgin's name was Mary. The angel greeted her and said, "The Lord has blessed you in a special way. He is with you."

Mary was very upset because of his words. She wondered what kind of greeting this could be. But the angel said to her, "Do not be afraid, Mary. God is very pleased with you. You will become pregnant and give birth to a son. You must call him Jesus. He will be great and will be called the Son of the Most High God. The Lord God will make him a king like his father David of long ago. The Son of the Most High God will rule forever over his people. They are from the family line of Jacob. That kingdom will never end."

"How can this happen?" Mary asked the angel. "I am a virgin."

The angel answered, "The Holy Spirit will come to you. The power of the Most High God will cover you. So the holy one that is born will be called the Son of God. Your relative Elizabeth will have a child even though she is old. People thought she could not have children. But she has been pregnant for six months now. That's because what God says will always come true."

"I serve the Lord," Mary answered. "May it happen to me just as you said it would." Then the angel left her.

⟨∽∞⟩

In those days, Caesar Augustus made a law. It required that a list be made of everyone in the whole Roman world. It was the first time a list was made of the people while Quirinius was governor of Syria. Everyone went to their own town to be listed.

So Joseph went also. He went from the town of Nazareth in Galilee to Judea. That is where Bethlehem, the town of David, was.

Joseph went there because he belonged to the family line of David. He went there with Mary to be listed. Mary was engaged to him. She was expecting a baby. While Joseph and Mary were there, the time came for the child to be born. She gave birth to her first baby. It was a boy. She wrapped him in large strips of cloth. Then she placed him in a manger. That's because there was no guest room where they could stay.

There were shepherds living out in the fields nearby. It was night, and they were taking care of their sheep. An angel of the Lord appeared to them. And the glory of the Lord shone around them. They were terrified. But the angel said to them, "Do not be afraid. I bring you good news. It will bring great joy for all the people. Today in the town of David a Savior has been born to you. He is the Messiah, the Lord. Here is how you will know I am telling you the truth. You will find a baby wrapped in strips of cloth and lying in a manger."

Suddenly a large group of angels from heaven also appeared. They were praising God. They said,

"May glory be given to God in the highest heaven!
And may peace be given to those he is pleased with on
    earth!"

The angels left and went into heaven. Then the shepherds said to one another, "Let's go to Bethlehem. Let's see this thing that has happened, which the Lord has told us about."

So they hurried off and found Mary and Joseph and the baby. The baby was lying in the manger. After the shepherds had seen him, they told everyone. They reported what the angel had said about this child. All who heard it were amazed at what the shepherds said to them. But Mary kept all these things like a secret treasure in her heart. She thought about them over and over. The shepherds returned. They gave glory and praise to God. Everything they had seen and heard was just as they had been told.

When the child was eight days old, he was circumcised. At the same time he was named Jesus. This was the name the angel had given him before his mother became pregnant.

Joseph and Mary did everything the Law of the Lord required.

Then they returned to Galilee. They went to their own town of Nazareth. And the child grew and became strong. He was very wise. He was blessed by God's grace.

⌇⌇⌇

Every year Jesus' parents went to Jerusalem for the Passover Feast. When Jesus was 12 years old, they went up to the feast as usual. After the feast was over, his parents left to go back home. The boy Jesus stayed behind in Jerusalem. But they were not aware of it. They thought he was somewhere in their group. So they traveled on for a day. Then they began to look for him among their relatives and friends. They did not find him. So they went back to Jerusalem to look for him. After three days they found him in the temple courtyard. He was sitting with the teachers. He was listening to them and asking them questions. Everyone who heard him was amazed at how much he understood. They also were amazed at his answers. When his parents saw him, they were amazed. His mother said to him, "Son, why have you treated us like this? Your father and I have been worried about you. We have been looking for you everywhere."

"Why were you looking for me?" he asked. "Didn't you know I had to be in my Father's house?" But they did not understand what he meant by that.

Then he went back to Nazareth with them, and he obeyed them. But his mother kept all these things like a secret treasure in her heart. Jesus became wiser and stronger. He also became more and more pleasing to God and to people.

⌇⌇⌇

Tiberius Caesar had been ruling for 15 years. Pontius Pilate was governor of Judea. Herod was the ruler of Galilee. His brother Philip was the ruler of Iturea and Traconitis. Lysanias was ruler of Abilene. Annas and Caiaphas were high priests. At that time God's word came to John, son of Zechariah, in the desert. He went into all the countryside around the Jordan River. There he preached that people should be baptized and turn away from their sins.

Then God would forgive them. Here is what is written in the book of Isaiah the prophet. It says,

"A messenger is calling out in the desert,
'Prepare the way for the Lord.
  Make straight paths for him.
  Every valley will be filled in.
  Every mountain and hill will be made level.
The crooked roads will become straight.
  The rough ways will become smooth.
  And all people will see God's salvation.'"

John spoke to the crowds coming to be baptized by him. He said, "You are like a nest of poisonous snakes! Who warned you to escape the coming of God's anger? Live in a way that shows you have turned away from your sins. And don't start saying to yourselves, 'Abraham is our father.' I tell you, God can raise up children for Abraham even from these stones. The ax is already lying at the roots of the trees. All the trees that don't produce good fruit will be cut down. They will be thrown into the fire."

"Then what should we do?" the crowd asked.

John answered, "Anyone who has extra clothes should share with the one who has none. And anyone who has extra food should do the same."

Even tax collectors came to be baptized. "Teacher," they asked, "what should we do?"

"Don't collect any more than you are required to," John told them.

Then some soldiers asked him, "And what should we do?"

John replied, "Don't force people to give you money. Don't bring false charges against people. Be happy with your pay."

The people were waiting. They were expecting something. They were all wondering in their hearts if John might be the Messiah. John answered them all, "I baptize you with water. But one who is more powerful than I am will come. I'm not good enough to untie the straps of his sandals. He will baptize you with the Holy Spirit and fire. His pitchfork is in his hand to toss the straw away from his threshing floor. He will gather the wheat into his barn. But he will burn up the husks with fire that can't be put out." John said many other things to warn the people. He also announced the good news to them.

When all the people were being baptized, Jesus was baptized too. And as he was praying, heaven was opened. The Holy Spirit came to rest on him in the form of a dove. A voice came from heaven. It said, "You are my Son, and I love you. I am very pleased with you." Jesus was about 30 years old when he began his special work for God and others. It was thought that he was the son of Joseph.

~~~

Jesus, full of the Holy Spirit, left the Jordan River. The Spirit led him into the desert. There the devil tempted him for 40 days. Jesus ate nothing during that time. At the end of the 40 days, he was hungry.

The devil said to him, "If you are the Son of God, tell this stone to become bread."

Jesus answered, "It is written, 'Man must not live only on bread.'"

Then the devil led Jesus up to a high place. In an instant, he showed Jesus all the kingdoms of the world. He said to Jesus, "I will give you all their authority and glory. It has been given to me, and I can give it to anyone I want to. If you worship me, it will all be yours."

Jesus answered, "It is written, 'Worship the Lord your God. He is the only one you should serve.'"

Then the devil led Jesus to Jerusalem. He had Jesus stand on the highest point of the temple. "If you are the Son of God," he said, "throw yourself down from here. It is written,

" 'The Lord will command his angels to take good care of you.
They will lift you up in their hands.
  Then you won't trip over a stone.'"

Jesus answered, "Scripture says, 'Do not test the Lord your God.'"

When the devil finished all this tempting, he left Jesus until a better time.

remember what you read

1. What is something you noticed for the first time?

_____

_____

_____

_____

2. What questions did you have?

_____

_____

_____

_____

3. Was there anything that bothered you?

_____

_____

_____

_____

4. What did you learn about loving God?

_____

_____

_____

_____

5. What did you learn about loving others?

_____

_____

_____

_____

LUKE-ACTS, PART 2

introduction to Luke-Acts, part 2

Jesus is all grown up. His job? Telling others that God's kingdom has come to earth. But he doesn't just talk about it. He shows it by doing all sorts of amazing things.

As you read, see if you notice what kind of people Jesus likes to hang out with. Does he stick to the popular crowd, or does he spend most of his time with outsiders—the poor, the sick, the hungry?

Jesus returned to Galilee in the power of the Holy Spirit. News about him spread through the whole countryside. He was teaching in their synagogues, and everyone praised him.

Jesus went to Nazareth, where he had been brought up. On the Sabbath day he went into the synagogue as he usually did. He stood up to read. And the scroll of Isaiah the prophet was handed to him. Jesus unrolled it and found the right place. There it is written,

"The Spirit of the Lord is on me.
He has anointed me
to announce the good news to poor people.
He has sent me to announce freedom for prisoners.
He has sent me so that the blind will see again.
He wants me to set free those who are treated badly.
And he has sent me to announce the year when he will set
his people free."

Then Jesus rolled up the scroll. He gave it back to the attendant and sat down. The eyes of everyone in the synagogue were staring at him. He began by saying to them, "Today this passage of Scripture is coming true as you listen."

ᴄ𝔶𝔶𝔶ᴐ

One day Jesus was standing by the Sea of Galilee. The people crowded around him and listened to the word of God. Jesus saw two boats at the edge of the water. They had been left there by the fishermen, who were washing their nets. He got into the boat that belonged to Simon. Jesus asked him to go out a little way from shore. Then he sat down in the boat and taught the people.

When he finished speaking, he turned to Simon. Jesus said, "Go out into deep water. Let down the nets so you can catch some fish."

Simon answered, "Master, we've worked hard all night and haven't caught anything. But because you say so, I will let down the nets."

When they had done so, they caught a large number of fish. There were so many that their nets began to break. So they motioned to their partners in the other boat to come and help them. They came and filled both boats so full that they began to sink.

When Simon Peter saw this, he fell at Jesus' knees. "Go away from me, Lord!" he said. "I am a sinful man!" He and everyone with him were amazed at the number of fish they had caught. So were James and John, the sons of Zebedee, who worked with Simon.

Then Jesus said to Simon, "Don't be afraid. From now on you will fish for people." So they pulled their boats up on shore. Then they left everything and followed him.

On one of those days, Jesus went out to a mountainside to pray. He spent the night praying to God. When morning came, he called for his disciples to come to him. He chose 12 of them and made them apostles. Here are their names.

Simon, whom Jesus named Peter, and his brother Andrew
James
John
Philip

Bartholomew
Matthew
Thomas
James, son of Alphaeus
Simon who was called the Zealot
Judas, son of James
and Judas Iscariot who would later hand Jesus over to his
  enemies

Jesus went down the mountain with them and stood on a level place. A large crowd of his disciples was there. A large number of other people were there too. They came from all over Judea, including Jerusalem. They also came from the coastland around Tyre and Sidon. They had all come to hear Jesus and to be healed of their sicknesses. People who were troubled by evil spirits were made well. Everyone tried to touch Jesus. Power was coming from him and healing them all.

Jesus looked at his disciples. He said to them,

"Blessed are you who are needy.
  God's kingdom belongs to you.
Blessed are you who are hungry now.
  You will be satisfied.
Blessed are you who are sad now.
  You will laugh.
Blessed are you when people hate you,
  when they have nothing to do with you
  and say bad things about you,
  and when they treat your name as something evil.
    They do all this because you are followers of the Son of
    Man.

"The prophets of long ago were treated the same way. When these things happen to you, be glad and jump for joy. You will receive many blessings in heaven.

"But here is what I tell you who are listening. Love your enemies.

Do good to those who hate you. Bless those who call down curses on you. And pray for those who treat you badly. Suppose someone slaps you on one cheek. Let them slap you on the other cheek as well. Suppose someone takes your coat. Don't stop them from taking your shirt as well. Give to everyone who asks you. And if anyone takes what belongs to you, don't ask to get it back. Do to others as you want them to do to you.

"Suppose you love those who love you. Should anyone praise you for that? Even sinners love those who love them. And suppose you do good to those who are good to you. Should anyone praise you for that? Even sinners do that. And suppose you lend money to those who can pay you back. Should anyone praise you for that? Even a sinner lends to sinners, expecting them to pay everything back. But love your enemies. Do good to them. Lend to them without expecting to get anything back. Then you will receive a lot in return. And you will be children of the Most High God. He is kind to people who are evil and are not thankful. So have mercy, just as your Father has mercy.

"If you do not judge other people, then you will not be judged. If you do not find others guilty, then you will not be found guilty. Forgive, and you will be forgiven. Give, and it will be given to you. A good amount will be poured into your lap. It will be pressed down, shaken together, and running over. The same amount you give will be measured out to you."

"You look at the bit of sawdust in your friend's eye. But you pay no attention to the piece of wood in your own eye. How can you say to your friend, 'Let me take the bit of sawdust out of your eye'? How can you say this while there is a piece of wood in your own eye? You pretender! First take the piece of wood out of your own eye. Then you will be able to see clearly to take the bit of sawdust out of your friend's eye.

"Why do you call me, 'Lord, Lord,' and still don't do what I say? Some people come and listen to me and do what I say. I will show you what they are like. They are like a man who builds a house. He digs down deep and sets it on solid rock. When a flood comes, the river rushes against the house. But the water can't shake it. The house is well built. But here is what happens when people listen to my words and do not obey them. They are like a man who builds a house on soft ground instead of solid rock. The moment the river rushes against that house, it falls down. It is completely destroyed."

⟳⟳⟳

Jesus finished saying all these things to the people who were listening. Then he entered Capernaum. There the servant of a Roman commander was sick and about to die. His master thought highly of him. The commander heard about Jesus. So he sent some elders of the Jews to him. He told them to ask Jesus to come and heal his servant. They came to Jesus and begged him, "This man deserves to have you do this. He loves our nation and has built our synagogue." So Jesus went with them.

When Jesus came near the house, the Roman commander sent friends to him. He told them to say, "Lord, don't trouble yourself. I am not good enough to have you come into my house. That is why I did not even think I was fit to come to you. But just say the word, and my servant will be healed. I myself am a man who is under authority. And I have soldiers who obey my orders. I tell this one, 'Go,' and he goes. I tell that one, 'Come,' and he comes. I say to my servant, 'Do this,' and he does it."

When Jesus heard this, he was amazed at the commander. Jesus turned to the crowd that was following him. He said, "I tell you, even in Israel I have not found anyone whose faith is so strong." Then the men who had been sent to Jesus returned to the house. They found that the servant was healed.

⟳⟳⟳

One day Jesus said to his disciples, "Let's go over to the other side of the lake." So they got into a boat and left. As they sailed, Jesus fell asleep. A storm came down on the lake. It was so bad that the boat was about to sink. They were in great danger.

The disciples went and woke Jesus up. They said, "Master! Master! We're going to drown!"

He got up and ordered the wind and the huge waves to stop. The storm quieted down. It was completely calm. "Where is your faith?" he asked his disciples.

They were amazed and full of fear. They asked one another, "Who is this? He commands even the winds and the waves, and they obey him."

When Jesus returned, a crowd welcomed him. They were all expecting him. Then a man named Jairus came. He was a synagogue leader. He fell at Jesus' feet and begged Jesus to come to his house. His only daughter was dying. She was about 12 years old. As Jesus was on his way, the crowds almost crushed him.

A woman was there who had a sickness that made her bleed. Her sickness had lasted for 12 years. No one could heal her. She came up behind Jesus and touched the edge of his clothes. Right away her bleeding stopped.

"Who touched me?" Jesus asked.

Everyone said they didn't do it. Then Peter said, "Master, the people are crowding and pushing against you."

But Jesus said, "Someone touched me. I know that power has gone out from me."

The woman realized that people would notice her. Shaking with fear, she came and fell at his feet. In front of everyone, she told why she had touched him. She also told how she had been healed in an instant. Then he said to her, "Dear woman, your faith has healed you. Go in peace."

While Jesus was still speaking, someone came from the house of Jairus. Jairus was the synagogue leader. "Your daughter is dead," the messenger said. "Don't bother the teacher anymore."

Hearing this, Jesus said to Jairus, "Don't be afraid. Just believe. She will be healed."

When he arrived at the house of Jairus, he did not let everyone go in with him. He took only Peter, John and James, and the child's father and mother. During this time, all the people were crying and sobbing loudly over the child. "Stop crying!" Jesus said. "She is not dead. She is sleeping."

They laughed at him. They knew she was dead. But he took her by the hand and said, "My child, get up!" Her spirit returned, and right away she stood up. Then Jesus told them to give her something to eat. Her parents were amazed. But Jesus ordered them not to tell anyone what had happened.

remember what you read

1. What is something you noticed for the first time?

_____

_____

_____

_____

2. What questions did you have?

_____

_____

_____

_____

3. Was there anything that bothered you?

_____

_____

_____

_____

4. What did you learn about loving God?

_____

_____

_____

_____

5. What did you learn about loving others?

_____

_____

_____

_____

LUKE-ACTS, PART 3

introduction to Luke-Acts, part 3

In our last reading of Luke's story, Jesus stayed close to home—
a place called Galilee. In today's reading, he sets out for Jerusalem,
the city where Jewish people worshiped God.

Along the way, Jesus teaches his followers many important things.
See how many of them you can remember after reading.

Jesus called together the 12 disciples. He gave them power and authority to drive out all demons and to heal sicknesses. Then he sent them out to announce God's kingdom and to heal those who were sick. He told them, "Don't take anything for the journey. Do not take a walking stick or a bag. Do not take any bread, money or extra clothes. When you are invited into a house, stay there until you leave town. Some people may not welcome you. If they don't, leave their town and shake the dust off your feet. This will be a witness against the people living there." So the 12 disciples left. They went from village to village. They announced the good news and healed people everywhere.

The disciples returned. They told Jesus what they had done. Then he took them with him. They went off by themselves to a town called Bethsaida. But the crowds learned about it and followed Jesus. He welcomed them and spoke to them about God's kingdom. He also healed those who needed to be healed.

Late in the afternoon the 12 disciples came to him. They said, "Send the crowd away. They can go to the nearby villages and countryside. There they can find food and a place to stay. There is nothing here."

Jesus replied, "You give them something to eat."

The disciples answered, "We have only five loaves of bread and two fish. We would have to go and buy food for all this crowd." About 5,000 men were there.

But Jesus said to his disciples, "Have them sit down in groups of about 50 each." The disciples did so, and everyone sat down. Jesus took the five loaves and the two fish. He looked up to heaven and gave thanks. He broke them into pieces. Then he gave them to the disciples to give to the people. All of them ate and were satisfied. The disciples picked up 12 baskets of leftover pieces.

⟊⟊⟊

The time grew near for Jesus to be taken up to heaven. So he made up his mind to go to Jerusalem. He sent messengers on ahead. They went into a Samaritan village to get things ready for him. But the people there did not welcome Jesus. That was because he was heading for Jerusalem. The disciples James and John saw this. They asked, "Lord, do you want us to call down fire from heaven to destroy them?" But Jesus turned and commanded them not to do it. Then Jesus and his disciples went on to another village.

One day an authority on the law stood up to test Jesus. "Teacher," he asked, "what must I do to receive eternal life?"

"What is written in the Law?" Jesus replied. "How do you understand it?"

He answered, " 'Love the Lord your God with all your heart and with all your soul. Love him with all your strength and with all your mind.' And, 'Love your neighbor as you love yourself.' "

"You have answered correctly," Jesus replied. "Do that, and you will live."

But the man wanted to make himself look good. So he asked Jesus, "And who is my neighbor?"

Jesus replied, "A man was going down from Jerusalem to Jericho. Robbers attacked him. They stripped off his clothes and beat him.

Then they went away, leaving him almost dead. A priest happened to be going down that same road. When he saw the man, he passed by on the other side. A Levite also came by. When he saw the man, he passed by on the other side too. But a Samaritan came to the place where the man was. When he saw the man, he felt sorry for him. He went to him, poured olive oil and wine on his wounds and bandaged them. Then he put the man on his own donkey. He brought him to an inn and took care of him. The next day he took out two silver coins. He gave them to the owner of the inn. 'Take care of him,' he said. 'When I return, I will pay you back for any extra expense you may have.'

"Which of the three do you think was a neighbor to the man who was attacked by robbers?"

The authority on the law replied, "The one who felt sorry for him."

Jesus told him, "Go and do as he did."

ᔆᔆᔆ

Jesus and his disciples went on their way. Jesus came to a village where a woman named Martha lived. She welcomed him into her home. She had a sister named Mary. Mary sat at the Lord's feet listening to what he said. But Martha was busy with all the things that had to be done. She came to Jesus and said, "Lord, my sister has left me to do the work by myself. Don't you care? Tell her to help me!"

"Martha, Martha," the Lord answered. "You are worried and upset about many things. But few things are needed. Really, only one thing is needed. Mary has chosen what is better. And it will not be taken away from her."

ᔆᔆᔆ

One day Jesus was praying in a certain place. When he finished, one of his disciples spoke to him. "Lord," he said, "teach us to pray, just as John taught his disciples."

Jesus said to them, "When you pray, this is what you should say.

" 'Father,
may your name be honored.
May your kingdom come.
Give us each day our daily bread.
Forgive us our sins,
   as we also forgive everyone who sins against us.
Keep us from falling into sin when we are tempted.' "

Then Jesus said to them, "Suppose you have a friend. You go to him at midnight and say, 'Friend, lend me three loaves of bread. A friend of mine on a journey has come to stay with me. I have no food to give him.' And suppose the one inside answers, 'Don't bother me. The door is already locked. My children and I are in bed. I can't get up and give you anything.' I tell you, that person will not get up. And he won't give you bread just because he is your friend. But because you keep bothering him, he will surely get up. He will give you as much as you need.

"So here is what I say to you. Ask, and it will be given to you. Search, and you will find. Knock, and the door will be opened to you. Everyone who asks will receive. The one who searches will find. And the door will be opened to the one who knocks."

Then Jesus spoke to his disciples. He said, "I tell you, do not worry. Don't worry about your life and what you will eat. And don't worry about your body and what you will wear. There is more to life than eating. There are more important things for the body than clothes. Think about the ravens. They don't plant or gather crops. They don't have any barns at all. But God feeds them. You are worth much more than birds! Can you add even one hour to your life by worrying? You can't do that very little thing. So why worry about the rest?

"Think about how the wild flowers grow. They don't work or make clothing. But here is what I tell you. Not even Solomon in his royal robes was dressed like one of those flowers. If that is how God dresses the wild grass, how much better will he dress you!

After all, the grass is here only today. Tomorrow it is thrown into the fire. Your faith is so small! Don't spend time thinking about what you will eat or drink. Don't worry about it. People who are ungodly run after all those things. Your Father knows that you need them. But put God's kingdom first. Then those other things will also be given to you.

"Little flock, do not be afraid. Your Father has been pleased to give you the kingdom. Sell what you own. Give to those who are poor. Provide purses for yourselves that will not wear out. Store up riches in heaven that will never be used up. There, no thief can come near it. There, no moth can destroy it. Your heart will be where your riches are.

Then Jesus asked, "What is God's kingdom like? What can I compare it to? It is like a mustard seed. Someone took the seed and planted it in a garden. It grew and became a tree. The birds sat in its branches."

Again he asked, "What can I compare God's kingdom to? It is like yeast that a woman used. She mixed it into 60 pounds of flour. The yeast worked its way all through the dough."

⁓⁓⁓

Then Jesus went through the towns and villages, teaching the people. He was on his way to Jerusalem.

One Sabbath day, Jesus went to eat in the house of a well-known Pharisee. While he was there, he was being carefully watched. In front of him was a man whose body was badly swollen. Jesus turned to the Pharisees and the authorities on the law. He asked them, "Is it breaking the Law to heal on the Sabbath day?" But they remained silent. So Jesus took hold of the man and healed him. Then he sent him away.

He asked them another question. He said, "Suppose one of you has a child or an ox that falls into a well on the Sabbath day. Wouldn't you pull it out right away?" And they had nothing to say.

Then Jesus spoke to his host. "Suppose you give a lunch or a dinner," he said. "Do not invite your friends, your brothers or sisters, or your relatives, or your rich neighbors. If you do, they may invite you to eat with them. So you will be paid back. But when you give a banquet, invite those who are poor. Also invite those who can't see or walk. Then you will be blessed. Your guests can't pay you back. But you will be paid back when those who are right with God rise from the dead."

One of the people at the table with Jesus heard him say those things. So he said to Jesus, "Blessed is the one who will eat at the feast in God's kingdom."

Jesus replied, "A certain man was preparing a great banquet. He invited many guests. Then the day of the banquet arrived. He sent his servant to those who had been invited. The servant told them, 'Come. Everything is ready now.'

"But they all had the same idea. They began to make excuses. The first one said, 'I have just bought a field. I have to go and see it. Please excuse me.'

"Another said, 'I have just bought five pairs of oxen. I'm on my way to try them out. Please excuse me.'

"Still another said, 'I just got married, so I can't come.'

"The servant came back and reported this to his master. Then the owner of the house became angry. He ordered his servant, 'Go out quickly into the streets and lanes of the town. Bring in those who are poor. Also bring those who can't see or walk.'

" 'Sir,' the servant said, 'what you ordered has been done. But there is still room.'

"Then the master told his servant, 'Go out to the roads. Go out to the country lanes. Make the people come in. I want my house to be full. I tell you, not one of those people who were invited will get a taste of my banquet.' "

remember what you read

1. What is something you noticed for the first time?

_____

_____

_____

_____

2. What questions did you have?

_____

_____

_____

_____

3. Was there anything that bothered you?

_____

_____

_____

_____

4. What did you learn about loving God?

_____

_____

_____

_____

5. What did you learn about loving others?

_____

_____

_____

_____

LUKE-ACTS, PART 4

introduction to Luke-Acts, part 4

Not everyone is happy about Jesus. The religious leaders were supposed to point people to God. But instead, they grew powerful and greedy. They actually kept people away from God.

Jesus is all about setting people free — which is the last thing some of the leaders want. Will they be able to get along? Or are things about to get very ugly?

✦✦✦

The tax collectors and sinners were all gathering around to hear Jesus. But the Pharisees and the teachers of the law were whispering among themselves. They said, "This man welcomes sinners and eats with them."

Then Jesus told them a story. He said, "Suppose one of you has 100 sheep and loses one of them. Won't he leave the 99 in the open country? Won't he go and look for the one lost sheep until he finds it? When he finds it, he will joyfully put it on his shoulders and go home. Then he will call his friends and neighbors together. He will say, 'Be joyful with me. I have found my lost sheep.' I tell you, it will be the same in heaven. There will be great joy when one sinner turns away from sin. Yes, there will be more joy than for 99 godly people who do not need to turn away from their sins.

Jesus continued, "There was a man who had two sons. The younger son spoke to his father. He said, 'Father, give me my share of the family property.' So the father divided his property between his two sons.

"Not long after that, the younger son packed up all he had. Then he left for a country far away. There he wasted his money on wild living. He spent everything he had. Then the whole country ran low on food. So the son didn't have what he needed. He went to work for someone who lived in that country. That person sent the son to the fields to feed the pigs. The son wanted to fill his stomach with the food the pigs were eating. But no one gave him anything.

"Then he began to think clearly again. He said, 'How many of my father's hired servants have more than enough food! But here I am dying from hunger! I will get up and go back to my father. I will say to him, "Father, I have sinned against heaven. And I have sinned against you. I am no longer fit to be called your son. Make me like one of your hired servants."' So he got up and went to his father.

"While the son was still a long way off, his father saw him. He was filled with tender love for his son. He ran to him. He threw his arms around him and kissed him.

"The son said to him, 'Father, I have sinned against heaven and against you. I am no longer fit to be called your son.'

"But the father said to his servants, 'Quick! Bring the best robe and put it on him. Put a ring on his finger and sandals on his feet. Bring the fattest calf and kill it. Let's have a feast and celebrate. This son of mine was dead. And now he is alive again. He was lost. And now he is found.' So they began to celebrate.

"The older son was in the field. When he came near the house, he heard music and dancing. So he called one of the servants. He asked him what was going on. 'Your brother has come home,' the servant replied. 'Your father has killed the fattest calf. He has done this because your brother is back safe and sound.'

"The older brother became angry. He refused to go in. So his father went out and begged him. But he answered his father, 'Look! All these years I've worked like a slave for you. I have always obeyed your orders. You never gave me even a young goat so I could celebrate with my friends. But this son of yours wasted your money with some prostitutes. Now he comes home. And for him you kill the fattest calf!'

" 'My son,' the father said, 'you are always with me. Everything I have is yours. But we had to celebrate and be glad. This brother of yours was dead. And now he is alive again. He was lost. And now he is found.' "

~~~

Jesus was on his way to Jerusalem. He traveled along the border between Samaria and Galilee. As he was going into a village, ten men met him. They had a skin disease. They were standing close by. And they called out in a loud voice, "Jesus! Master! Have pity on us!"

Jesus saw them and said, "Go. Show yourselves to the priests." While they were on the way, they were healed.

When one of them saw that he was healed, he came back. He praised God in a loud voice. He threw himself at Jesus' feet and thanked him. The man was a Samaritan.

Jesus asked, "Weren't all ten healed? Where are the other nine? Didn't anyone else return and give praise to God except this outsider?" Then Jesus said to him, "Get up and go. Your faith has healed you."

~~~

Once the Pharisees asked Jesus when God's kingdom would come. He replied, "The coming of God's kingdom is not something you can see. People will not say, 'Here it is.' Or, 'There it is.' That's because God's kingdom is among you."

~~~

People were also bringing babies to Jesus. They wanted him to place his hands on the babies. When the disciples saw this, they told the people to stop. But Jesus asked the children to come to him. "Let the little children come to me," he said. "Don't keep them away. God's kingdom belongs to people like them. What I'm about to tell you is true. Anyone who will not receive God's kingdom like a little child will never enter it."

A certain ruler asked Jesus a question. "Good teacher," he said, "what must I do to receive eternal life?"

"Why do you call me good?" Jesus answered. "No one is good except God. You know what the commandments say. 'Do not commit adultery. Do not commit murder. Do not steal. Do not be a false witness. Honor your father and mother.' "

"I have obeyed all those commandments since I was a boy," the ruler said.

When Jesus heard this, he said to him, "You are still missing one thing. Sell everything you have. Give the money to those who are poor. You will have treasure in heaven. Then come and follow me."

When the ruler heard this, he became very sad. He was very rich. Jesus looked at him. Then he said, "How hard it is for rich people to enter God's kingdom! Is it hard for a camel to go through the eye of a needle? It is even harder for someone who is rich to enter God's kingdom!"

Those who heard this asked, "Then who can be saved?"

Jesus replied, "Things that are impossible with people are possible with God."

Peter said to him, "We have left everything we had in order to follow you!"

"What I'm about to tell you is true," Jesus said to them. "Has anyone left home or wife or husband or brothers or sisters or parents or children for God's kingdom? They will receive many times as much in this world. In the world to come they will receive eternal life."

Jesus took the 12 disciples to one side. He told them, "We are going up to Jerusalem. Everything that the prophets wrote about the Son of Man will come true. He will be handed over to the Gentiles. They will make fun of him. They will laugh at him and spit on him. They will whip him and kill him. On the third day, he will rise from the dead!"

The disciples did not understand any of this. Its meaning was hidden from them. So they didn't know what Jesus was talking about.

჻჻჻

Jesus entered Jericho and was passing through. A man named Zacchaeus lived there. He was a chief tax collector and was very rich. Zacchaeus wanted to see who Jesus was. But he was a short man. He could not see Jesus because of the crowd. So he ran ahead and climbed a sycamore-fig tree. He wanted to see Jesus, who was coming that way.

Jesus reached the spot where Zacchaeus was. He looked up and said, "Zacchaeus, come down at once. I must stay at your house today." So Zacchaeus came down at once and welcomed him gladly.

All the people saw this. They began to whisper among themselves. They said, "Jesus has gone to be the guest of a sinner."

But Zacchaeus stood up. He said, "Look, Lord! Here and now I give half of what I own to those who are poor. And if I have cheated anybody out of anything, I will pay it back. I will pay back four times the amount I took."

Jesus said to Zacchaeus, "Today salvation has come to your house. You are a member of Abraham's family line. The Son of Man came to look for the lost and save them."

჻჻჻

After Jesus had said this, he went on ahead. He was going up to Jerusalem. He approached Bethphage and Bethany. The hill there was called the Mount of Olives. Jesus sent out two of his disciples. He said to them, "Go to the village ahead of you. As soon as you get there, you will find a donkey's colt tied up. No one has ever ridden it. Untie it and bring it here. Someone may ask you, 'Why are you untying it?' If so, say, 'The Lord needs it.'"

Those who were sent ahead went and found the young donkey. It was there just as Jesus had told them. They were untying the colt when its owners came. The owners asked them, "Why are you untying the colt?"

They replied, "The Lord needs it."

Then the disciples brought the colt to Jesus. They threw their coats on the young donkey and put Jesus on it. As he went along, people spread their coats on the road.

Jesus came near the place where the road goes down the Mount of Olives. There the whole crowd of disciples began to praise God with joy. In loud voices they praised him for all the miracles they had seen. They shouted,

"Blessed is the king who comes in the name of the Lord!"

"May there be peace and glory in the highest heaven!"

Some of the Pharisees in the crowd spoke to Jesus. "Teacher," they said, "tell your disciples to stop!"

"I tell you," he replied, "if they keep quiet, the stones will cry out."

He approached Jerusalem. When he saw the city, he began to weep. He said, "I wish you had known today what would bring you peace! But now it is hidden from your eyes. The days will come when your enemies will arrive. They will build a wall of dirt up against your city. They will surround you and close you in on every side. You didn't recognize the time when God came to you. So your enemies will smash you to the ground. They will destroy you and all the people inside your walls. They will not leave one stone on top of another."

Then Jesus entered the temple courtyard. He began to drive out those who were selling there. He told them, "It is written that the Lord said, 'My house will be a house where people can pray.' But you have made it a 'den for robbers.' "

Every day Jesus was teaching at the temple. But the chief priests and the teachers of the law were trying to kill him. So were the leaders among the people. But they couldn't find any way to do it. All the people were paying close attention to his words.

remember what you read

1. What is something you noticed for the first time?

_____

_____

_____

_____

2. What questions did you have?

_____

_____

_____

_____

3. Was there anything that bothered you?

_____

_____

_____

_____

4. What did you learn about loving God?

_____

_____

_____

_____

5. What did you learn about loving others?

_____

_____

_____

_____

LUKE-ACTS, PART 5

introduction to Luke-Acts, part 5

In the final reading from Luke's story, Jesus arrives in Jerusalem. The religious leaders have had enough. They're ready to put a stop to him—for good.

So they come up with a plan to have Jesus killed. The question is, who gets the last laugh?

The Feast of Unleavened Bread, called the Passover, was near. The chief priests and the teachers of the law were looking for a way to get rid of Jesus. They were afraid of the people. Then Satan entered Judas, who was called Iscariot. Judas was one of the 12 disciples. He went to the chief priests and the officers of the temple guard. He talked with them about how he could hand Jesus over to them. They were delighted and agreed to give him money. Judas accepted their offer. He watched for the right time to hand Jesus over to them. He wanted to do it when no crowd was around.

Jesus went out as usual to the Mount of Olives. His disciples followed him. When they reached the place, Jesus spoke. "Pray that you won't fall into sin when you are tempted," he said to them. Then he went a short distance away from them. There he got down on his knees and prayed. He said, "Father, if you are willing, take this cup of suffering away from me. But do what you want, not what I want." An angel from heaven appeared to Jesus and gave him strength. Because he was very sad and troubled, he prayed even harder. His sweat was like drops of blood falling to the ground.

After that, he got up from prayer and went back to the disciples. He found them sleeping. They were worn out because they were very sad. "Why are you sleeping?" he asked them. "Get up! Pray that you won't fall into sin when you are tempted."

While Jesus was still speaking, a crowd came up. The man named Judas was leading them. He was one of the 12 disciples. Judas approached Jesus to kiss him. But Jesus asked him, "Judas, are you handing over the Son of Man with a kiss?"

Jesus' followers saw what was going to happen. So they said, "Lord, should we use our swords against them?" One of them struck the slave of the high priest and cut off his right ear.

But Jesus answered, "Stop this!" And he touched the man's ear and healed him.

Then Jesus spoke to the chief priests, the officers of the temple guard, and the elders. They had all come for him. "Am I leading a band of armed men against you?" he asked. "Do you have to come with swords and clubs? Every day I was with you in the temple courtyard. And you didn't lay a hand on me. But this is your hour. This is when darkness rules."

Then the men arrested Jesus and led him away. They took him into the high priest's house. Peter followed from far away. Some people there started a fire in the middle of the courtyard. Then they sat down together. Peter sat down with them. A female servant saw him sitting there in the firelight. She looked closely at him. Then she said, "This man was with Jesus."

But Peter said he had not been with him. "Woman, I don't know him," he said.

A little later someone else saw Peter. "You also are one of them," he said.

"No," Peter replied. "I'm not!"

About an hour later, another person spoke up. "This fellow must have been with Jesus," he said. "He is from Galilee."

Peter replied, "Man, I don't know what you're talking about!" Just as he was speaking, the rooster crowed. The Lord turned and looked right at Peter. Then Peter remembered what the Lord had spoken to him. "The rooster will crow today," Jesus had said. "Before it does, you will say three times that you don't know me." Peter went outside. He broke down and cried.

⟨⟨⟨∘

At dawn the elders of the people met together. These included the chief priests and the teachers of the law. Jesus was led to them. "If you are the Messiah," they said, "tell us."

Jesus answered, "If I tell you, you will not believe me. And if I asked you, you would not answer. But from now on, the Son of Man will be seated at the right hand of the mighty God."

They all asked, "Are you the Son of God then?"

He replied, "You say that I am."

Then they said, "Why do we need any more witnesses? We have heard it from his own lips."

Then the whole group got up and led Jesus off to Pilate. They began to bring charges against Jesus. They said, "We have found this man misleading our people. He is against paying taxes to Caesar. And he claims to be Messiah, a king."

Pilate called together the chief priests, the rulers and the people. He said to them, "You brought me this man. You said he was turning the people against the authorities. I have questioned him in front of you. I have found no basis for your charges against him. Herod hasn't either. So he sent Jesus back to us. As you can see, Jesus has done nothing that is worthy of death. So I will just have him whipped and let him go."

But the whole crowd shouted, "Kill this man! But let Barabbas go!" Barabbas had been thrown into prison. He had taken part in a struggle in the city against the authorities. He had also committed murder.

Pilate wanted to let Jesus go. So he made an appeal to the crowd again. But they kept shouting, "Crucify him! Crucify him!"

Pilate spoke to them for the third time. "Why?" he asked. "What wrong has this man done? I have found no reason to have him put to death. So I will just have him whipped and let him go."

But with loud shouts they kept calling for Jesus to be crucified. The people's shouts won out. So Pilate decided to give them what they wanted. He set free the man they asked for. The man had been thrown in prison for murder and for fighting against the authorities. Pilate handed Jesus over to them so they could carry out their plans.

⟨⟨⟨

Two other men were also led out with Jesus to be killed. Both of them had broken the law. The soldiers brought them to the place called the Skull. There they nailed Jesus to the cross. He hung between the two criminals. One was on his right and one was on his left. Jesus said, "Father, forgive them. They don't know what they are doing." The soldiers divided up his clothes by casting lots.

The people stood there watching. The rulers even made fun of Jesus. They said, "He saved others. Let him save himself if he is God's Messiah, the Chosen One."

The soldiers also came up and poked fun at him. They offered him wine vinegar. They said, "If you are the king of the Jews, save yourself."

A written sign had been placed above him. It read,

THIS IS THE KING OF THE JEWS.

One of the criminals hanging there made fun of Jesus. He said, "Aren't you the Messiah? Save yourself! Save us!"

But the other criminal scolded him. "Don't you have any respect for God?" he said. "Remember, you are under the same sentence of death. We are being punished fairly. We are getting just what our actions call for. But this man hasn't done anything wrong."

Then he said, "Jesus, remember me when you come into your kingdom."

Jesus answered him, "What I'm about to tell you is true. Today you will be with me in paradise."

It was now about noon. Then darkness covered the whole land until three o'clock. The sun had stopped shining. The temple curtain was torn in two. Jesus called out in a loud voice, "Father, into your hands I commit my life." After he said this, he took his last breath.

The Roman commander saw what had happened. He praised God and said, "Jesus was surely a man who did what was right." The people had gathered to watch this sight. When they saw what happened, they felt very sad. Then they went away. But all those who knew Jesus stood not very far away, watching these things. They included the women who had followed him from Galilee.

∽ꙮ∾

It was very early in the morning on the first day of the week. The women took the spices they had prepared. Then they went to the tomb. They found the stone rolled away from it. When they entered the tomb, they did not find the body of the Lord Jesus. They were wondering about this. Suddenly two men in clothes as bright as lightning stood beside them. The women were terrified. They bowed down with their faces to the ground. Then the men said to them, "Why do you look for the living among the dead? Jesus is not here! He has risen! Remember how he told you he would rise. It was while he was still with you in Galilee. He said, 'The Son of Man must be handed over to sinful people. He must be nailed to a cross. On the third day he will rise from the dead.'" Then the women remembered Jesus' words.

They came back from the tomb. They told all these things to the 11 apostles and to all the others. Mary Magdalene, Joanna, Mary the mother of James, and the others with them were the ones who told the apostles. But the apostles did not believe the women. Their words didn't make any sense to them. But Peter got up and ran to the tomb. He bent over and saw the strips of linen lying by themselves. Then he went away, wondering what had happened.

The disciples were still talking about this when Jesus himself suddenly stood among them. He said, "May you have peace!"

They were surprised and terrified. They thought they were seeing a ghost. Jesus said to them, "Why are you troubled? Why do you have doubts in your minds? Look at my hands and my feet. It's really me! Touch me and see. A ghost does not have a body or bones. But you can see that I do."

After he said that, he showed them his hands and feet. But they still did not believe it. They were amazed and filled with joy. So Jesus asked them, "Do you have anything here to eat?" They gave him a piece of cooked fish. He took it and ate it in front of them.

Jesus said to them, "This is what I told you while I was still with you. Everything written about me in the Law of Moses, the Prophets and the Psalms must come true."

Then he opened their minds so they could understand the Scriptures. He told them, "This is what is written. The Messiah will suffer. He will rise from the dead on the third day. His followers will preach in his name. They will tell others to turn away from their sins and be forgiven. People from every nation will hear it, beginning at Jerusalem. You have seen these things with your own eyes. I am going to send you what my Father has promised. But for now, stay in the city. Stay there until you have received power from heaven."

Jesus led his disciples out to the area near Bethany. Then he lifted up his hands and blessed them. While he was blessing them, he left them. He was taken up into heaven. Then they worshiped him. With great joy, they returned to Jerusalem. Every day they went to the temple, praising God.

remember what you read

1. What is something you noticed for the first time?

_____

_____

_____

_____

2. What questions did you have?

_____

_____

_____

_____

3. Was there anything that bothered you?

_____

_____

_____

_____

4. What did you learn about loving God?

_____

_____

_____

_____

5. What did you learn about loving others?

_____

_____

_____

_____

LUKE-ACTS, PART 6

introduction to Luke-Acts, part 6

Luke, the doctor who shared the story of Jesus, wrote another book for his friend Theophilus. This one is called the book of Acts. Why? Well, because it records the acts or activities of those who helped spread the message of Jesus.

After Jesus rose from the dead and went up to heaven, more and more people began following him. It started in the city of Jerusalem, but then it spread all over the Roman Empire.

Near the beginning of Acts, God's Holy Spirit comes to the disciples in Jerusalem, and the church is born. Then followers of Jesus spread to the area around Jerusalem. They start reaching out to non-Jewish people called Gentiles.

Then followers of Jesus take the good news even farther—all the way to the Roman province of Asia. They keep going until they reach Europe.

Finally, they reach the capital city, Rome—the most powerful city in the world. And so God's invitation is extended to people all over.

After reading the story of Acts, go online with a parent and find a map showing the Roman Empire during the first century AD. See if you can locate some of the places you hear about in this story. You could even print the map and draw a circle around Jerusalem—then bigger circles around Palestine, the province of Asia, and Europe—so you can see for yourself just how far the good news about Jesus spread in a few years' time.

The apostles returned to Jerusalem from the hill called the Mount of Olives. It is just over half a mile from the city. When they arrived, they went upstairs to the room where they were staying. Here is a list of those who were there.

Peter, John, James and Andrew,
Philip and Thomas,
Bartholomew and Matthew,
James son of Alphaeus, Simon the Zealot and Judas son of
   James

They all came together regularly to pray. The women joined them too. So did Jesus' mother Mary and his brothers.

When the day of Pentecost came, all the believers gathered in one place. Suddenly a sound came from heaven. It was like a strong wind blowing. It filled the whole house where they were sitting. They saw something that looked like fire in the shape of tongues. The flames separated and came to rest on each of them. All of them were filled with the Holy Spirit. They began to speak in languages they had not known before. The Spirit gave them the ability to do this.

Godly Jews from every country in the world were staying in Jerusalem. A crowd came together when they heard the sound. They were bewildered because each of them heard their own language being spoken. The crowd was really amazed. They asked, "Aren't all these people who are speaking Galileans? Then why do we each hear them speaking in our own native language? We are Parthians, Medes and Elamites. We live in Mesopotamia, Judea and Cappadocia. We are from Pontus, Asia, Phrygia and Pamphylia. Others of us are from Egypt and the parts of Libya near Cyrene. Still others are visitors from Rome. Some of the visitors are Jews. Others have accepted the Jewish faith. Also, Cretans and Arabs are here. We hear all these people speaking about God's wonders in our own languages!" They were amazed and bewildered. They asked one another, "What does this mean?"

But some people in the crowd made fun of the believers. "They've had too much wine!" they said.

Then Peter stood up with the 11 apostles. In a loud voice he spoke to the crowd. "My fellow Jews," he said, "let me explain this to you. All of you who live in Jerusalem, listen carefully to what I say. You think these people are drunk. But they aren't. It's only nine o'clock in the morning! No, here is what the prophet Joel meant. He said,

" 'In the last days, God says,
I will pour out my Holy Spirit on all people.
Your sons and daughters will prophesy.
  Your young men will see visions.
  Your old men will have dreams.
In those days, I will pour out my Spirit on my servants.
  I will pour out my Spirit on both men and women.
  When I do, they will prophesy.
I will show wonders in the heavens above.
  I will show signs on the earth below.
  There will be blood and fire and clouds of smoke.
The sun will become dark.
  The moon will turn red like blood.
  This will happen before the coming of the great and
    glorious day of the Lord.
Everyone who calls
  on the name of the Lord will be saved.'

"Fellow Israelites, listen to this! Jesus of Nazareth was a man who had God's approval. God did miracles, wonders and signs among you through Jesus. You yourselves know this. Long ago God planned that Jesus would be handed over to you. With the help of evil people, you put Jesus to death. You nailed him to the cross. But God raised him from the dead. He set him free from the suffering of death. It wasn't possible for death to keep its hold on Jesus.

When the people heard this, it had a deep effect on them. They said to Peter and the other apostles, "Brothers, what should we do?"

Peter replied, "All of you must turn away from your sins and be baptized in the name of Jesus Christ. Then your sins will be forgiven. You will receive the gift of the Holy Spirit. The promise is for you and your children. It is also for all who are far away. It is for all whom the Lord our God will choose."

Peter said many other things to warn them. He begged them, "Save yourselves from these evil people." Those who accepted his message were baptized. About 3,000 people joined the believers that day.

◯◯◯

The believers studied what the apostles taught. They shared their lives together. They ate and prayed together. Everyone was amazed at what God was doing. They were amazed when the apostles performed many wonders and signs. All the believers were together. They shared everything they had. They sold property and other things they owned. They gave to anyone who needed something. Every day they met together in the temple courtyard. They ate meals together in their homes. Their hearts were glad and sincere. They praised God. They were respected by all the people. Every day the Lord added to their group those who were being saved.

◯◯◯

One day Peter and John were going up to the temple. It was three o'clock in the afternoon. It was the time for prayer. A man unable to walk was being carried to the temple gate called Beautiful. He had been that way since he was born. Every day someone put him near the gate. There he would beg from people going into the temple courtyards. He saw that Peter and John were about to enter. So he asked them for money. Peter looked straight at him, and so did John. Then Peter said, "Look at us!" So the man watched them closely. He expected to get something from them.

Peter said, "I don't have any silver or gold. But I'll give you what I do have. In the name of Jesus Christ of Nazareth, get up and walk." Then Peter took him by the right hand and helped him up. At once the man's feet and ankles became strong. He jumped to his feet and began to walk. He went with Peter and John into the temple courtyards. He walked and jumped and praised God. All the people saw him walking and praising God. They recognized him as the same man who used to sit and beg at the temple gate called Beautiful. They were filled with wonder. They were amazed at what had happened to him.

The man was holding on to Peter and John. All the people were amazed. They came running to them at the place called Solomon's Porch. When Peter saw this, he said, "Fellow Israelites, why does this surprise you? Why do you stare at us? It's not as if we've made this man walk by our own power or godliness. The God of our fathers, Abraham, Isaac and Jacob, has done this. God has brought glory to Jesus, who serves him. But you handed Jesus over to be killed. Pilate had decided to let him go. But you spoke against Jesus when he was in Pilate's court. You spoke against the Holy and Blameless One. You asked for a murderer to be set free instead. You killed the one who gives life. But God raised him from the dead. We are witnesses of this. This man whom you see and know was made strong because of faith in Jesus' name. Faith in Jesus has healed him completely. You can see it with your own eyes.

༄ঞ৵

All the believers were agreed in heart and mind. They didn't claim that anything they had was their own. Instead, they shared everything they owned. With great power the apostles continued their teaching. They were telling people that the Lord Jesus had risen from the dead. And God's grace was working powerfully in all of them. So there were no needy persons among them. From time to time, those who owned land or houses sold them. They brought the money from the sales. They put it down at the apostles' feet. It was then given out to anyone who needed it.

A man named Ananias and his wife, Sapphira, also sold some land. He kept part of the money for himself. Sapphira knew he had kept it. He brought the rest of it and put it down at the apostles' feet.

Then Peter said, "Ananias, why did you let Satan fill your heart? He made you lie to the Holy Spirit. You have kept some of the money you received for the land. Didn't the land belong to you before it was sold? After it was sold, you could have used the money as you wished. What made you think of doing such a thing? You haven't lied just to people. You've also lied to God."

When Ananias heard this, he fell down and died. All who heard what had happened were filled with fear. Some young men came and wrapped up his body. They carried him out and buried him.

About three hours later, the wife of Ananias came in. She didn't know what had happened. Peter asked her, "Tell me. Is this the price you and Ananias sold the land for?"

"Yes," she said. "That's the price."

Peter asked her, "How could you agree to test the Spirit of the Lord? Listen! You can hear the steps of the men who buried your husband. They are at the door. They will carry you out also."

At that moment she fell down at Peter's feet and died. Then the young men came in. They saw that Sapphira was dead. So they carried her out and buried her beside her husband. The whole church and all who heard about these things were filled with fear.

The apostles did many signs and wonders among the people. All the believers used to meet together at Solomon's Porch. No outsider dared to join them. But the people thought highly of them. More and more men and women believed in the Lord. They joined the other believers. So people brought those who were sick into the streets. They placed them on beds and mats. They hoped that at least Peter's shadow might fall on some of them as he walked by. Crowds even gathered from the towns around Jerusalem. They brought their sick people. They also brought those who were suffering because of evil spirits. All of them were healed.

⟨∫∫∫⟩

In those days the number of believers was growing. The Greek Jews complained about the non-Greek Jews. They said that the widows of the Greek Jews were not being taken care of. They weren't getting their fair share of food each day. So the 12 apostles gathered all the believers together. They said, "It wouldn't be right for us to give up teaching God's word. And we'd have to stop teaching to wait on tables. Brothers and sisters, choose seven of your men. They must be known as men who are wise and full of the

Holy Spirit. We will turn this important work over to them. Then we can give our attention to prayer and to teaching God's word." This plan pleased the whole group. They chose Stephen. He was full of faith and of the Holy Spirit. Philip, Procorus, Nicanor, Timon and Parmenas were chosen too. The group also chose Nicolas from Antioch. He had accepted the Jewish faith. The group brought them to the apostles. Then the apostles prayed and placed their hands on them.

So God's word spread. The number of believers in Jerusalem grew quickly. Also, a large number of priests began to obey Jesus' teachings.

remember what you read

1. What is something you noticed for the first time?

_____

_____

_____

_____

2. What questions did you have?

_____

_____

_____

_____

3. Was there anything that bothered you?

_____

_____

_____

_____

4. What did you learn about loving God?

_____

_____

_____

_____

5. What did you learn about loving others?

_____

_____

_____

_____

LuKE-ACTS, PART 7

introduction to Luke-Acts, part 7

The early church got off to an amazing start. Every day, more and more people were becoming followers of Jesus. The entire city of Jerusalem was buzzing with excitement.

Then some powerful people started attacking the church. Believers ran for their lives. But notice what happens when they spread out from Jerusalem. And be sure to pay special attention to a man named Saul, one of the church's most powerful enemies.

೧ೲಾ

Stephen was full of God's grace and power. He did great wonders and signs among the people. But members of the group called the Synagogue of the Freedmen began to oppose him. Some of them were Jews from Cyrene and Alexandria. Others were Jews from Cilicia and Asia Minor. They all began to argue with Stephen. But he was too wise for them. That's because the Holy Spirit gave Stephen wisdom whenever he spoke.

Then in secret they talked some men into lying about Stephen. They said, "We heard Stephen speak evil things against Moses and against God."

So the people were stirred up. The elders and the teachers of the law were stirred up too. They arrested Stephen and brought him to the Sanhedrin. They found witnesses who were willing to tell lies. These liars said, "This fellow never stops speaking against this holy place. He also speaks against the law. We have heard him say that this Jesus of Nazareth will destroy this place. He says Jesus will change the practices that Moses handed down to us."

All who were sitting in the Sanhedrin looked right at Stephen. They saw that his face was like the face of an angel. He looked up to heaven and saw God's glory. He saw Jesus standing at God's right hand. "Look!" he said. "I see heaven open. The Son of Man is standing at God's right hand." When the Sanhedrin heard this, they covered their ears. They yelled at the top of their voices. They all rushed at him. They dragged him out of the city. They began to throw stones at him to kill him. The people who had brought false charges against Stephen took off their coats. They placed them at the feet of a young man named Saul.

While the members of the Sanhedrin were throwing stones at Stephen, he prayed. "Lord Jesus, receive my spirit," he said. Then he fell on his knees. He cried out, "Lord! Don't hold this sin against them!" When he had said this, he died.

And Saul had agreed with the Sanhedrin that Stephen should die.

On that day the church in Jerusalem began to be attacked and treated badly. All except the apostles were scattered throughout Judea and Samaria. Godly Jews buried Stephen. They mourned deeply for him. But Saul began to destroy the church. He went from house to house. He dragged away men and women and put them in prison.

⌒⌒⌒⌒

Meanwhile, Saul continued to oppose the Lord's followers. He said they would be put to death. He went to the high priest. He asked the priest for letters to the synagogues in Damascus. He wanted to find men and women who belonged to the Way of Jesus. The letters would allow him to take them as prisoners to Jerusalem. On his journey, Saul approached Damascus. Suddenly a light from heaven flashed around him. He fell to the ground. He heard a voice speak to him, "Saul! Saul! Why are you opposing me?"

"Who are you, Lord?" Saul asked.

"I am Jesus," he replied. "I am the one you are opposing. Now get up and go into the city. There you will be told what you must do."

The men traveling with Saul stood there. They weren't able to speak. They had heard the sound. But they didn't see anyone. Saul got up from the ground. He opened his eyes, but he couldn't see. So they led him by the hand into Damascus. For three days he was blind. He didn't eat or drink anything.

In Damascus there was a believer named Ananias. The Lord called out to him in a vision. "Ananias!" he said.

"Yes, Lord," he answered.

The Lord told him, "Go to the house of Judas on Straight Street. Ask for a man from Tarsus named Saul. He is praying. In a vision Saul has seen a man come and place his hands on him. That man's name is Ananias. In the vision, Ananias placed his hands on Saul so he could see again."

"Lord," Ananias answered, "I've heard many reports about this man. They say he has done great harm to your holy people in Jerusalem. Now he has come here to arrest all those who worship you. The chief priests have given him authority to do this."

But the Lord said to Ananias, "Go! I have chosen this man to work for me. He will announce my name to the Gentiles and to their kings. He will also announce my name to the people of Israel. I will show him how much he must suffer for me."

Then Ananias went to the house and entered it. He placed his hands on Saul. "Brother Saul," he said, "you saw the Lord Jesus. He appeared to you on the road as you were coming here. He has sent me so that you will be able to see again. You will be filled with the Holy Spirit." Right away something like scales fell from Saul's eyes. And he could see again. He got up and was baptized. After eating some food, he got his strength back.

Saul spent several days with the believers in Damascus. Right away he began to preach in the synagogues. He taught that Jesus is the Son of God. All who heard him were amazed. They asked, "Isn't he the man who caused great trouble in Jerusalem? Didn't he make trouble for those who worship Jesus? Hasn't he come here to take them as prisoners to the chief priests?" But Saul grew more and more powerful. The Jews living in Damascus couldn't believe what was happening. Saul proved to them that Jesus is the Messiah.

Then the church throughout Judea, Galilee and Samaria enjoyed a time of peace. The church was strengthened and grew larger. That's because they worshiped the Lord and the Holy Spirit helped them.

⌇

A man named Cornelius lived in Caesarea. He was a Roman commander in the Italian Regiment. Cornelius and all his family were faithful and worshiped God. He gave freely to people who were in need. He prayed to God regularly. One day about three o'clock in the afternoon he had a vision. He saw clearly an angel of God. The angel came to him and said, "Cornelius!"

Cornelius was afraid. He stared at the angel. "What is it, Lord?" he asked.

The angel answered, "Your prayers and gifts to poor people are like an offering to God. So he has remembered you. Now send men to Joppa. Have them bring back a man named Simon. He is also called Peter. He is staying with another Simon, a man who works with leather. His house is by the sea."

The angel who spoke to him left. Then Cornelius called two of his servants. He also called a godly soldier who was one of his attendants. He told them everything that had happened. Then he sent them to Joppa.

The men sent by Cornelius found Simon's house. Then Peter invited the men into the house to be his guests.

The next day Peter went with the three men. Some of the believers from Joppa went along. The following day he arrived in Caesarea. Cornelius was expecting them. He had called together his relatives and close friends. When Peter entered the house, Cornelius met him. As a sign of respect, he fell at Peter's feet. But Peter made him get up. "Stand up," he said. "I am only a man myself."

As he was talking with Cornelius, Peter went inside. There he found a large group of people. He said to them, "You know that it is against our law for a Jew to enter a Gentile home. A Jew shouldn't have any close contact with a Gentile. But God has shown me that I should not say anyone is not pure and 'clean.' So when you sent for me, I came without asking any questions.

"I now realize how true it is that God treats everyone the same," he said. "He accepts people from every nation. He accepts anyone who has respect for him and does what is right. You know the message God sent to the people of Israel. It is the good news of peace through Jesus Christ. He is Lord of all. You know what has happened all through the area of Judea. It started in Galilee after John preached about baptism. You know how God anointed Jesus of Nazareth with the Holy Spirit and with power. Jesus went around doing good. He healed all who were under the devil's power. God was with him.

"We are witnesses of everything he did in the land of the Jews and in Jerusalem. They killed him by nailing him to a cross. But on the third day God raised him from the dead. God allowed Jesus to be seen. But he wasn't seen by all the people. He was seen only by us. We are witnesses whom God had already chosen. We ate and drank with him after he rose from the dead. He commanded us to preach to the people. He told us to tell people that he is the one appointed by God to judge the living and the dead. All the prophets tell about him. They say that all who believe in him have their sins forgiven through his name."

The apostles and the believers all through Judea heard that Gentiles had also received God's word. They said, "So then, God has allowed even Gentiles to turn away from their sins. He did this so that they could live."

ᘓᎶᎶᏅ

About this time, King Herod arrested some people who belonged to the church. He planned to make them suffer greatly. He had James killed with a sword. James was John's brother. Herod saw that the death of James pleased some Jews. So he arrested Peter also. This happened during the Feast of Unleavened Bread. After Herod arrested Peter, he put him in prison. Peter was placed under guard. He was watched by four groups of four soldiers each. Herod planned to put Peter on public trial. It would take place after the Passover Feast.

So Peter was kept in prison. But the church prayed hard to God for him.

It was the night before Herod was going to bring him to trial. Peter was sleeping between two soldiers. Two chains held him there. Lookouts stood guard at the entrance. Suddenly an angel of the Lord appeared. A light shone in the prison cell. The angel struck Peter on his side. Peter woke up. "Quick!" the angel said. "Get up!" The chains fell off Peter's wrists. Then the angel said to him, "Put on your clothes and sandals." Peter did so. "Put on your coat," the angel told him. "Follow me." Peter followed him out of the prison. But he had no idea that what the angel was doing was really happening. He thought he was seeing a vision. They passed the first and second guards. Then they came to the iron gate leading to the city. It opened for them by itself. They went through it. They walked the length of one street. Suddenly the angel left Peter.

When Peter understood what had happened, he went to Mary's house. Mary was the mother of John Mark. Many people had gathered in her home. They were praying there. Peter knocked at the outer entrance. A servant named Rhoda came to answer the door. She recognized Peter's voice. She was so excited that she ran back without opening the door. "Peter is at the door!" she exclaimed.

Peter kept on knocking. When they opened the door and saw him, they were amazed. Peter motioned with his hand for them to be quiet. He explained how the Lord had brought him out of prison. "Tell James and the other brothers and sisters about this," he said. Then he went to another place.

But God's word continued to spread and many people believed the message.

remember what you read

1. What is something you noticed for the first time?

_____

_____

_____

_____

2. What questions did you have?

_____

_____

_____

_____

3. Was there anything that bothered you?

_____

_____

_____

_____

4. What did you learn about loving God?

_____

_____

_____

_____

5. What did you learn about loving others?

_____

_____

_____

_____

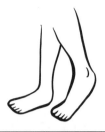

introduction to Luke-Acts, part 8

*In our last reading of Acts, Saul got a new job. He's not putting
Christians in jail anymore; he's telling people about Jesus!*

*In today's reading, Saul gets a new name, too. He and his friend
Barnabas travel around, sharing the good news with everyone they
meet, Jews and non-Jews. They say that Jesus loves everyone, no
matter where they come from or what they look like.*

*But there are some people who don't like this idea. See what
happens when an argument breaks out over who to include in the
church.*

*As you read, you might also notice that Luke, the writer of Acts,
starts saying "we" a lot. That's because partway through this reading,
Luke joins up with Paul as one of his traveling companions.*

Barnabas and Saul were sent on their way by the Holy Spirit.
They went down to Seleucia. From there they sailed to Cyprus.
They arrived at Salamis. There they preached God's word in the
Jewish synagogues. John was with them as their helper.

From Paphos, Paul and his companions sailed to Perga in Pamphylia. There John Mark left them and returned to Jerusalem.
From Perga they went on to Pisidian Antioch. On the Sabbath day
they entered the synagogue and sat down. The Law and the Prophets were read aloud. Then the leaders of the synagogue sent word
to Paul and his companions. They said, "Brothers, do you have any
words of instruction for the people? If you do, please speak."

Paul stood up and motioned with his hand. Then he said, "Fellow Israelites, and you Gentiles who worship God, listen to me! The God of Israel chose our people who lived long ago. He blessed them greatly while they were in Egypt. With his mighty power he led them out of that country. He put up with their behavior for about 40 years in the desert. And he destroyed seven nations in Canaan. Then he gave the land to his people as their rightful share. All this took about 450 years.

"After this, God gave them judges until the time of Samuel the prophet. Then the people asked for a king. He gave them Saul, son of Kish. Saul was from the tribe of Benjamin. He ruled for 40 years. God removed him and made David their king. Here is God's witness about him. 'David, son of Jesse, is a man dear to my heart,' he said. 'David will do everything I want him to do.'

"From this man's family line God has brought to Israel the Savior Jesus. This is what he had promised. Before Jesus came, John preached that we should turn away from our sins and be baptized. He preached this to all Israel. John was coming to the end of his work. 'Who do you suppose I am?' he said. 'I am not the one you are looking for. But there is someone coming after me. I am not good enough to untie his sandals.'

"Listen, fellow children of Abraham! Listen, you Gentiles who worship God! This message of salvation has been sent to us. The people of Jerusalem and their rulers did not recognize Jesus. By finding him guilty, they made the prophets' words come true. These are read every Sabbath day. The people and their rulers had no reason at all for sentencing Jesus to death. But they asked Pilate to have him killed. They did everything that had been written about Jesus. Then they took him down from the cross. They laid him in a tomb. But God raised him from the dead. For many days he was seen by those who had traveled with him from Galilee to Jerusalem. Now they are telling our people about Jesus.

"We are telling you the good news. What God promised our people long ago he has done for us, their children. He has raised up Jesus. This is what is written in the second Psalm. It says,

" 'You are my son.
Today I have become your father.'

On the next Sabbath day, almost the whole city gathered. They gathered to hear the word of the Lord. When the Jews saw the crowds, they became very jealous. They began to disagree with what Paul was saying. They said evil things against him. Then Paul and Barnabas answered them boldly. "We had to speak God's word to you first," they said. "But you don't accept it. You don't think you are good enough for eternal life. So now we are turning to the Gentiles. This is what the Lord has commanded us to do. He said,

" 'I have made you a light for the Gentiles.
You will bring salvation to the whole earth.' "

When the Gentiles heard this, they were glad. They honored the word of the Lord. All who were appointed for eternal life believed.

❧

Certain people came down from Judea to Antioch. Here is what they were teaching the believers. "Moses commanded you to be circumcised," they said. "If you aren't, you can't be saved." But Paul and Barnabas didn't agree with this. They argued strongly with them. So Paul and Barnabas were appointed to go up to Jerusalem. Some other believers were chosen to go with them. They were told to ask the apostles and elders about this question. The church sent them on their way. They traveled through Phoenicia and Samaria. There they told how the Gentiles had turned to God. This news made all the believers very glad. When they arrived in Jerusalem, the church welcomed them. The apostles and elders welcomed them too. Then Paul and Barnabas reported everything God had done through them.

Some of the believers were Pharisees. They stood up and said, "The Gentiles must be circumcised. They must obey the law of Moses."

The apostles and elders met to consider this question. After they had talked it over, Peter got up and spoke to them. "Brothers," he said, "you know that some time ago God chose me. He appointed me to take the good news to the Gentiles. He wanted them to hear the good news and believe. God knows the human heart. By giving the Holy Spirit to the Gentiles, he showed that he accepted them. He did the same for them as he had done for us. God showed that there is no difference between us and them. That's because he made their hearts pure because of their faith. Now then, why are you trying to test God? You test him when you put a heavy load on the shoulders of Gentiles. Our people of long ago couldn't carry that load. We can't either. No! We believe we are saved through the grace of our Lord Jesus. The Gentiles are saved in the same way."

Everyone became quiet as they listened to Barnabas and Paul. They were telling about the signs and wonders God had done through them among the Gentiles.

Then the apostles, the elders and the whole church decided what to do. They would choose some of their own men who were leaders among the believers. They would send them to Antioch with Paul and Barnabas. So they chose Judas Barsabbas and Silas. They were leaders among the believers.

So the men were sent down to Antioch. Judas and Silas were prophets. They said many things to give strength and hope to the believers.

෴

Some time later Paul spoke to Barnabas. "Let's go back to all the towns where we preached the word of the Lord," he said. "Let's visit the believers and see how they are doing." Barnabas wanted to take John Mark with them. But Paul didn't think it was wise to take him. Mark had deserted them in Pamphylia. He hadn't continued with them in their work. Barnabas and Paul strongly disagreed with each other. So they went their separate ways. Barnabas took Mark and sailed for Cyprus. But Paul chose Silas. The believers asked the Lord to give his grace to Paul and Silas as they went. Paul traveled through Syria and Cilicia. He gave strength to the churches there.

Paul came to Derbe. Then he went on to Lystra. A believer named Timothy lived there. His mother was Jewish and a believer. His father was a Greek. The believers at Lystra and Iconium said good things about Timothy. Paul wanted to take him along on the journey. So he circumcised Timothy because of the Jews who lived in that area. They all knew that Timothy's father was a Greek. Paul and his companions traveled from town to town. They reported what the apostles and elders in Jerusalem had decided. The people were supposed to obey what was in the report. So the churches were made strong in the faith. The number of believers grew every day.

༒༒

Paul and his companions traveled all through the area of Phrygia and Galatia. The Holy Spirit had kept them from preaching the word in Asia Minor. They came to the border of Mysia. From there they tried to enter Bithynia. But the Spirit of Jesus would not let them. So they passed by Mysia. Then they went down to Troas. During the night Paul had a vision. He saw a man from Macedonia standing and begging him. "Come over to Macedonia!" the man said. "Help us!" After Paul had seen the vision, we got ready at once to leave for Macedonia. We decided that God had called us to preach the good news there.

At Troas we got into a boat. We sailed straight for Samothrace. The next day we went on to Neapolis. From there we traveled to Philippi, a Roman colony. It is an important city in that part of Macedonia. We stayed there several days.

One day we were going to the place of prayer. On the way we were met by a female slave. She had a spirit that helped her tell people what was going to happen. She earned a lot of money for her owners by doing this. She followed Paul and the rest of us around. She shouted, "These men serve the Most High God. They are telling you how to be saved." She kept this up for many days. Finally Paul became upset. Turning around, he spoke to the spirit that was in her. "In the name of Jesus Christ," he said, "I command you to come out of her!" At that very moment the spirit left the woman.

Her owners realized that their hope of making money was gone. So they grabbed Paul and Silas. They dragged them into the market place to face the authorities. They brought them to the judges. "These men are Jews," her owners said. "They are making trouble in our city. They are suggesting practices that are against Roman law. These are practices we can't accept or take part in."

The crowd joined the attack against Paul and Silas. The judges ordered that Paul and Silas be stripped and beaten with rods. They were whipped without mercy. Then they were thrown into prison. The jailer was commanded to guard them carefully. When he received these orders, he put Paul and Silas deep inside the prison. He fastened their feet so they couldn't get away.

About midnight Paul and Silas were praying. They were also singing hymns to God. The other prisoners were listening to them. Suddenly there was a powerful earthquake. It shook the prison from top to bottom. All at once the prison doors flew open. Everyone's chains came loose. The jailer woke up. He saw that the prison doors were open. He pulled out his sword and was going to kill himself. He thought the prisoners had escaped. "Don't harm yourself!" Paul shouted. "We are all here!"

The jailer called out for some lights. He rushed in, shaking with fear. He fell down in front of Paul and Silas. Then he brought them out. He asked, "Sirs, what must I do to be saved?"

They replied, "Believe in the Lord Jesus. Then you and everyone living in your house will be saved." They spoke the word of the Lord to him. They also spoke to all the others in his house. At that hour of the night, the jailer took Paul and Silas and washed their wounds. Right away he and everyone who lived with him were baptized. The jailer brought them into his house. He set a meal in front of them. He and everyone who lived with him were filled with joy. They had become believers in God.

remember what you read

1. What is something you noticed for the first time?

_____

_____

_____

_____

2. What questions did you have?

_____

_____

_____

_____

3. Was there anything that bothered you?

_____

_____

_____

_____

4. What did you learn about loving God?

_____

_____

_____

_____

5. What did you learn about loving others?

_____

_____

_____

_____

LUKE-ACTS, PART 9

introduction to Luke-Acts, part 9

Paul spent two years in the city of Ephesus, telling people about Jesus. But he had even bigger plans. He wanted to take the good news to Rome, the capital city of the mighty Roman Empire.

❧

Paul took the road to Ephesus. When he arrived, he found some believers there.

Paul entered the synagogue. There he spoke boldly for three months. He gave good reasons for believing the truth about God's kingdom. But some of them wouldn't listen. They refused to believe. In public they said evil things about the Way of Jesus. So Paul left them. He took the believers with him. Each day he talked with people in the lecture hall of Tyrannus. This went on for two years. So all the Jews and Greeks who lived in Asia Minor heard the word of the Lord.

God did amazing miracles through Paul. Even handkerchiefs and aprons that had touched him were taken to those who were sick. When this happened, their sicknesses were healed and evil spirits left them.

Some Jews went around driving out evil spirits. They tried to use the name of the Lord Jesus to set free those who were controlled by demons. They said, "In Jesus' name I command you to come out. He is the Jesus that Paul is preaching about." Seven sons of Sceva were doing this. Sceva was a Jewish chief priest. One day the evil spirit answered them, "I know Jesus. And I know about Paul.

But who are you?" Then the man who had the evil spirit jumped on Sceva's sons. He overpowered them all. He gave them a terrible beating. They ran out of the house naked and bleeding.

The Jews and Greeks living in Ephesus heard about this. They were all overcome with fear. They held the name of the Lord Jesus in high honor. Many who believed now came and openly admitted what they had done. A number of those who had practiced evil magic brought their scrolls together. They set them on fire out in the open. They added up the value of the scrolls. The scrolls were worth more than someone could earn in two lifetimes. The word of the Lord spread everywhere. It became more and more powerful.

❦

After all this had happened, Paul decided to go to Jerusalem. He went through Macedonia and Achaia. "After I have been to Jerusalem," he said, "I must visit Rome also." He sent Timothy and Erastus, two of his helpers, to Macedonia. But he stayed a little longer in Asia Minor.

At that time many people became very upset about the Way of Jesus. There was a man named Demetrius who made things out of silver. He made silver models of the temple of the goddess Artemis. He brought in a lot of business for the other skilled workers there. One day he called them together. He also called others who were in the same kind of business. "My friends," he said, "you know that we make good money from our work. You have seen and heard what this fellow Paul is doing. He has talked to large numbers of people here in Ephesus. Almost everywhere in Asia Minor he has led people away from our gods. He says that the gods made by human hands are not gods at all. Our work is in danger of losing its good name. People's faith in the temple of the great goddess Artemis will be weakened. Now she is worshiped all over Asia Minor and the whole world. But soon she will be robbed of her greatness."

When they heard this, they became very angry. They began shouting, "Great is Artemis of the Ephesians!" Soon people were making trouble in the whole city. They all rushed into the theater. They dragged Gaius and Aristarchus along with them. These two men had come with Paul from Macedonia. Paul wanted to appear in front of the crowd. But the believers wouldn't let him. Some of the officials in Asia Minor were friends of Paul. They sent him a message, begging him not to go into the theater.

The crowd didn't know what was going on. Some were shouting one thing and some another. Most of the people didn't even know why they were there. The Jews in the crowd pushed Alexander to the front. They tried to tell him what to say. But he motioned for them to be quiet. He was about to give the people reasons for his actions. But then they realized that he was a Jew. So they all shouted the same thing for about two hours. "Great is Artemis of the Ephesians!" they yelled.

The city clerk quieted the crowd down. "People of Ephesus!" he said. "The city of Ephesus guards the temple of the great Artemis. The whole world knows this. They know that Ephesus guards her statue, which fell from heaven. These facts can't be questioned. So calm down. Don't do anything foolish. These men haven't robbed any temples. They haven't said evil things against our female god. But you have brought them here anyhow. Demetrius and the other skilled workers may feel they have been wronged by someone. Let them bring charges. The courts are open. We have our governors. Is there anything else you want to bring up? Settle it in a court of law. As it is, we are in danger of being charged with a crime. We could be charged with causing all this trouble today. There is no reason for it. So we wouldn't be able to explain what has happened." After he said this, he sent the people away.

⸱ᘐᘐᘐ⸱

All the trouble came to an end. Then Paul sent for the believers. After encouraging them, he said goodbye. He then left for Macedonia. He traveled through that area, speaking many words of hope to the people. Finally he arrived in Greece. There he stayed for three months. He was just about to sail for Syria. But some Jews were making plans against him. So he decided to go back through

Macedonia. Sopater, son of Pyrrhus, from Berea went with him. Aristarchus and Secundus from Thessalonica, Gaius from Derbe, and Timothy went too. Tychicus and Trophimus from Asia Minor also went with him. These men went on ahead. They waited for us at Troas. But we sailed from Philippi after the Feast of Unleavened Bread. Five days later we joined the others at Troas. We stayed there for seven days.

On the first day of the week we met to break bread and eat together. Paul spoke to the people. He kept on talking until midnight because he planned to leave the next day. There were many lamps in the room upstairs where we were meeting. A young man named Eutychus was sitting in a window. He sank into a deep sleep as Paul talked on and on. Sound asleep, Eutychus fell from the third floor. When they picked him up from the ground, he was dead. Paul went down and threw himself on the young man. He put his arms around him. "Don't be alarmed," he told them. "He's alive!" Then Paul went upstairs again. He broke bread and ate with them. He kept on talking until daylight. Then he left. The people took the young man home. They were greatly comforted because he was alive.

◌⟨⟩◌

We went on ahead to the ship. We sailed for Assos. There we were going to take Paul on board. He had planned it this way because he wanted to go to Assos by land. So he met us there. We took him on board and went on to Mitylene. The next day we sailed from there. We arrived near Chios. The day after that we crossed over to Samos. We arrived at Miletus the next day. Paul had decided to sail past Ephesus. He didn't want to spend time in Asia Minor. He was in a hurry to get to Jerusalem. If he could, he wanted to be there by the day of Pentecost.

From Miletus, Paul sent for the elders of the church at Ephesus. When they arrived, he spoke to them. "You know how I lived the whole time I was with you," he said. "From the first day I came into Asia Minor, I served the Lord with tears and without pride. I served him when I was greatly tested. I was tested by the evil plans of the Jews who disagreed with me. You know that nothing has kept me from preaching whatever would help you. I have taught you in public and from house to house. I have told both Jews and Greeks that they must turn away from their sins to God. They must have faith in our Lord Jesus.

"Now I am going to Jerusalem. The Holy Spirit compels me. I don't know what will happen to me there. I only know that in every city the Spirit warns me. He tells me that I will face prison and suffering. But my life means nothing to me. My only goal is to finish the race. I want to complete the work the Lord Jesus has given me. He wants me to tell others about the good news of God's grace.

"I have spent time with you preaching about the kingdom. I know that none of you will ever see me again. So I tell you today that I am not guilty if any of you don't believe. I haven't let anyone keep me from telling you everything God wants you to do. Keep watch over yourselves. Keep watch over all the believers. The Holy Spirit has made you leaders over them. Be shepherds of God's church. He bought it with his own blood. I know that after I leave, wild wolves will come in among you. They won't spare any of the sheep. Even men from your own people will rise up and twist the truth. They want to get the believers to follow them. So be on your guard! Remember that for three years I never stopped warning you. Night and day I warned each of you with tears.

Paul finished speaking. Then he got down on his knees with all of them and prayed. They all wept as they hugged and kissed him. Paul had said that they would never see him again. That's what hurt them the most. Then they went with him to the ship.

remember what you read

1. What is something you noticed for the first time?

_____

_____

_____

_____

2. What questions did you have?

_____

_____

_____

_____

3. Was there anything that bothered you?

_____

_____

_____

_____

4. What did you learn about loving God?

_____

_____

_____

_____

5. What did you learn about loving others?

_____

_____

_____

_____

LUKE-ACTS, PART 10

introduction to Luke-Acts, part 10

Paul had lots of enemies who wanted him dead. In today's reading, they hatch their plan to put a stop to him once and for all. Pay attention to what happens when Paul is arrested, and notice how he uses the situation to realize his dream of preaching in Rome.

When we arrived in Jerusalem, the brothers and sisters gave us a warm welcome. The next day Paul and the rest of us went to see James. All the elders were there. Paul greeted them. Then he reported everything God had done among the Gentiles through his work.

Some Jews from Asia Minor saw Paul at the temple. They stirred up the whole crowd and grabbed Paul. "Fellow Israelites, help us!" they shouted. "This is the man who teaches everyone in all places against our people. He speaks against our law and against this holy place. Besides, he has brought Greeks into the temple. He has made this holy place 'unclean.'" They said this because they had seen Trophimus the Ephesian in the city with Paul. They thought Paul had brought him into the temple.

The whole city was stirred up. People came running from all directions. They grabbed Paul and dragged him out of the temple. Right away the temple gates were shut. The people were trying to kill Paul. But news reached the commander of the Roman troops. He heard that people were making trouble in the whole city of

Jerusalem. Right away he took some officers and soldiers with him. They ran down to the crowd. The people causing the trouble saw the commander and his soldiers. So they stopped beating Paul.

The commander came up and arrested Paul. He ordered him to be held with two chains. Then he asked who Paul was and what he had done. Some in the crowd shouted one thing, some another. But the commander couldn't get the facts because of all the noise. But then the mob became so wild that he had to be carried by the soldiers. The crowd that followed kept shouting, "Get rid of him!"

They shouted and threw off their coats. They threw dust into the air. So the commanding officer ordered that Paul be taken into the fort. He gave orders for Paul to be whipped and questioned. He wanted to find out why the people were shouting at him like this. A commander was standing there as they stretched Paul out to be whipped. Paul said to him, "Does the law allow you to whip a Roman citizen who hasn't even been found guilty?"

When the commander heard this, he went to the commanding officer and reported it. "What are you going to do?" the commander asked. "This man is a Roman citizen."

Right away those who were about to question him left. Even the officer was alarmed. He realized that he had put Paul, a Roman citizen, in chains.

The commanding officer wanted to find out exactly what the Jews had against Paul. So the next day he let Paul out of prison. He ordered a meeting of the chief priests and all the members of the Sanhedrin. Then he brought Paul and had him stand in front of them.

The people arguing were getting out of control. The commanding officer was afraid that Paul would be torn to pieces by them. So he ordered the soldiers to go down and take him away from them by force. The officer had told them to bring Paul into the fort.

The next night the Lord stood near Paul. He said, "Be brave! You have told people about me in Jerusalem. You must do the same in Rome."

The next morning some Jews gathered secretly to make plans against Paul. They made a promise to themselves. They promised that they would not eat or drink anything until they killed him. More than 40 men took part in this plan. They went to the chief priests and the elders. They said, "We have made a special promise to God. We will not eat anything until we have killed Paul. Now then, you and the Sanhedrin must make an appeal to the commanding officer. Ask him to bring Paul to you. Pretend you want more facts about his case. We are ready to kill him before he gets here."

But Paul's nephew heard about this plan. So he went into the fort and told Paul.

Then Paul called one of the commanders. He said to him, "Take this young man to the commanding officer. He has something to tell him." So the commander took Paul's nephew to the officer.

The commander said, "Paul, the prisoner, sent for me. He asked me to bring this young man to you. The young man has something to tell you."

The commanding officer took the young man by the hand. He spoke to him in private. "What do you want to tell me?" the officer asked.

He said, "Some Jews have agreed to ask you to bring Paul to the Sanhedrin tomorrow. They will pretend they want more facts about him. Don't give in to them. More than 40 of them are waiting in hiding to attack him. They have promised that they will not eat or drink anything until they have killed him. They are ready now. All they need is for you to bring Paul to the Sanhedrin."

The commanding officer let the young man go. But he gave him a warning. "Don't tell anyone you have reported this to me," he said.

Then the commanding officer called for two of his commanders. He ordered them, "Gather a company of 200 soldiers, 70 horsemen and 200 men armed with spears. Get them ready to go to Caesarea at nine o'clock tonight. Provide horses for Paul so that he may be taken safely to Governor Felix."

꩜

Two years passed. Porcius Festus took the place of Felix. But Felix wanted to do the Jews a favor. So he left Paul in prison.

Three days after Festus arrived, he went up from Caesarea to Jerusalem. There the chief priests and the Jewish leaders came to Festus. They brought their charges against Paul. They tried very hard to get Festus to have Paul taken to Jerusalem. They asked for this as a favor. They were planning to hide and attack Paul along the way. They wanted to kill him. Festus answered, "Paul is being held at Caesarea. Soon I'll be going there myself. Let some of your leaders come with me. If the man has done anything wrong, they can bring charges against him there."

Festus spent eight or ten days in Jerusalem with them. Then he went down to Caesarea. The next day he called the court together. He ordered Paul to be brought to him. When Paul arrived, the Jews who had come down from Jerusalem stood around him. They brought many strong charges against him. But they couldn't prove that these charges were true.

Then Paul spoke up for himself. He said, "I've done nothing wrong against the law of the Jews or against the temple. I've done nothing wrong against Caesar."

But Festus wanted to do the Jews a favor. So he said to Paul, "Are you willing to go up to Jerusalem? Are you willing to go on trial there? Are you willing to face these charges in my court?"

Paul answered, "I'm already standing in Caesar's court. This is where I should go on trial. I haven't done anything wrong to the Jews. You yourself know that very well. If I am guilty of anything worthy of death, I'm willing to die. But the charges brought against me by these Jews are not true. No one has the right to hand me over to them. I make my appeal to Caesar!"

Festus talked it over with the members of his court. Then he said, "You have made an appeal to Caesar. To Caesar you will go!"

∽∬∽

It was decided that we would sail for Italy. Paul and some other prisoners were handed over to a Roman commander named

Julius. He belonged to the Imperial Guard. We boarded a ship from Adramyttium. It was about to sail for ports along the coast of Asia Minor. We headed out to sea. Aristarchus was with us. He was a Macedonian from Thessalonica.

A gentle south wind began to blow. The ship's crew thought they saw their chance to leave safely. So they pulled up the anchor and sailed along the shore of Crete. Before very long, a wind blew down from the island. It had the force of a hurricane. It was called the Northeaster. The ship was caught by the storm. We could not keep it sailing into the wind. So we gave up and were driven along by the wind. We passed the calmer side of a small island called Cauda. We almost lost the lifeboat that was tied to the side of the ship. So the men lifted the lifeboat on board. Then they tied ropes under the ship itself to hold it together. They were afraid it would get stuck on the sandbars of Syrtis. So they lowered the sea anchor and let the ship be driven along. We took a very bad beating from the storm. The next day the crew began to throw the ship's contents overboard. On the third day, they even threw the ship's tools and supplies overboard with their own hands. The sun and stars didn't appear for many days. The storm was terrible. So we gave up all hope of being saved.

The men had not eaten for a long time. Paul stood up in front of them. "Men," he said, "you should have taken my advice not to sail from Crete. Then you would have avoided this harm and loss. Now I beg you to be brave. Not one of you will die. Only the ship will be destroyed. I belong to God and serve him. Last night his angel stood beside me. The angel said, 'Do not be afraid, Paul. You must go on trial in front of Caesar. God has shown his grace by sparing the lives of all those sailing with you.' Men, continue to be brave. I have faith in God. It will happen just as he told me. But we must run the ship onto the beach of some island."

When daylight came, they saw a bay with a sandy beach. They didn't recognize the place. But they decided to run the ship onto the beach if they could. So they cut the anchors loose and left them in the sea. At the same time, they untied the ropes that held the rudders. They lifted the sail at the front of the ship to the wind. Then they headed for the beach. But the ship hit a sandbar. So the front of it got stuck and wouldn't move. The back of the ship was broken to pieces by the pounding of the waves.

The soldiers planned to kill the prisoners. They wanted to keep them from swimming away and escaping. But the commander wanted to save Paul's life. So he kept the soldiers from carrying out their plan. He ordered those who could swim to jump overboard first and swim to land. The rest were supposed to get there on boards or other pieces of the ship. That is how everyone reached land safely.

When we were safe on shore, we found out that the island was called Malta. The people of the island were unusually kind. It was raining and cold. So they built a fire and welcomed all of us. When we were ready to sail, they gave us the supplies we needed.

After three months we headed out to sea. When we got to Rome, Paul was allowed to live by himself. But a soldier guarded him.

For two whole years Paul stayed there in a house he rented. He welcomed all who came to see him. He preached boldly about God's kingdom. He taught people about the Lord Jesus Christ. And no one could keep him from teaching and preaching about these things.

remember what you read

1. What is something you noticed for the first time?

_____

_____

_____

_____

2. What questions did you have?

_____

_____

_____

_____

3. Was there anything that bothered you?

_____

_____

_____

_____

4. What did you learn about loving God?

_____

_____

_____

_____

5. What did you learn about loving others?

_____

_____

_____

_____

1-2 THESSALONIANS

introduction to 1 Thessalonians

In this reading, we'll read some letters written by the apostle Paul. We first met Paul in the book of Acts, as he traveled all over, telling people about Jesus.

Paul wrote many letters to believers in different places. Sometimes he wrote to encourage them, challenge them, or answer questions they had.

Two of Paul's letters were written to believers living in a place called Thessalonica. The people there were called Thessalonians, which is how these two letters, 1 and 2 Thessalonians, got their names.

Paul was good friends with the believers in Thessalonica. In his first letter, he says how thankful he is that they've stayed true to their faith. Even though others were making it hard for them, they were still following Jesus. Paul teaches them how to keep strong in their faith. He tells them to love one another, work hard, and always keep praying to God.

Paul also explains what happens to believers who die before Jesus comes back to earth. They are not lost, Paul says, because Jesus will raise them from the dead when he comes back!

As you read, see if you notice what else Paul says about the day Jesus will come back, when it might happen, and what it will be like.

∽᷍ᕙᕈ᷍∾

I, Paul, am writing this letter. Silas and Timothy join me in writing.

We are sending this letter to you, the members of the church in Thessalonica. You belong to God the Father and the Lord Jesus Christ.

May grace and peace be given to you.

We always thank God for all of you. We keep on praying for you. We remember you when we pray to our God and Father. Your work is produced by your faith. Your service is the result of your love. Your strength to continue comes from your hope in our Lord Jesus Christ.

Brothers and sisters, you are loved by God. We know that he has chosen you. Our good news didn't come to you only in words. It came with power. It came with the Holy Spirit's help. He gave us complete faith in what we were preaching. You know how we lived among you for your good. We and the Lord were your examples. You followed us. You welcomed our message even when you were suffering terribly. You welcomed it with the joy the Holy Spirit gives. So you became a model to all the believers in the lands of Macedonia and Achaia. The Lord's message rang out from you. That was true not only in Macedonia and Achaia. Your faith in God has also become known everywhere. So we don't have to say anything about it. The believers themselves report the kind of welcome you gave us. They tell about how you turned away from statues of gods. And you turned to serve the living and true God. They tell about how you are waiting for his Son to come from heaven. God raised him from the dead. He is Jesus. He saves us from God's anger, and his anger is sure to come.

We couldn't wait any longer. So we thought it was best to be left by ourselves in Athens. We sent our brother Timothy to give you strength and hope in your faith. He works together with us in God's service to spread the good news about Christ. We sent him so that no one would be upset by times of testing. You know very well that we have to go through times of testing. In fact, when we were with you, here is what we kept telling you. We were telling you that our enemies would make us suffer. As you know very well, it has turned out that way. That's the reason I sent someone to find out about your faith. I couldn't wait any longer. I was afraid that Satan had tempted you in some way. Then our work among you would have been useless.

But Timothy has come to us from you just now. He has brought good news about your faith and love. He has told us that you always have happy memories of us. He has also said that you desire to see us, just as we desire to see you. Brothers and sisters, in all our trouble and suffering your faith encouraged us. Now we really live, because you are standing firm in the Lord. How can we thank God enough for you? We thank God because of all the joy we have in his presence. We have this joy because of you. Night and day we pray very hard that we will see you again. We want to give you what is missing in your faith.

❦

We don't need to write to you about your love for one another. God himself has taught you to love one another. In fact, you do love all God's family all around Macedonia. Brothers and sisters, we are asking you to love one another more and more. And do everything you can to live a quiet life. You should mind your own business. And work with your hands, just as we told you to. Then unbelievers will have respect for your everyday life. And you won't have to depend on anyone.

❦

Brothers and sisters, we want you to know what happens to those who die. We don't want you to mourn, as other people do. They mourn because they don't have any hope. We believe that Jesus died and rose again. When he returns, many who believe in him will have died already. We believe that God will bring them back with Jesus. This agrees with what the Lord has said. When the Lord comes, many of us will still be alive. We tell you that we will certainly not go up before those who have died. The Lord himself will come down from heaven. We will hear a loud command. We will hear the voice of the leader of the angels. We will hear a blast from God's trumpet. Many who believe in Christ will have died already. They will rise first. After that, we who are still alive and are left will be caught up together with them. We will be taken up in the clouds. We will meet the Lord in the air. And we will be with him forever. So encourage one another with these words of comfort.

⌇

Brothers and sisters, we don't have to write to you about times and dates. You know very well how the day of the Lord will come. It will come like a thief in the night. People will be saying that everything is peaceful and safe. Then suddenly they will be destroyed. It will happen like birth pains coming on a pregnant woman. None of the people will escape.

Brothers and sisters, you are not in darkness. So that day should not surprise you as a thief would. All of you are children of the light. You are children of the day. We don't belong to the night. We don't belong to the darkness. So let us not be like the others. They are asleep. Instead, let us be wide awake and in full control of ourselves. Those who sleep, sleep at night. Those who get drunk, get drunk at night. But we belong to the day. So let us control ourselves. Let us put on our chest the armor of faith and love. Let us put on the hope of salvation like a helmet. God didn't choose us to receive his anger. He chose us to receive salvation because of what our Lord Jesus Christ has done. Jesus died for us. Some will be alive when he comes. Others will be dead. Either way, we will live together with him. So encourage one another with the hope you have. Build each other up. In fact, that's what you are doing.

⌇

Always be joyful. Never stop praying. Give thanks no matter what happens. God wants you to thank him because you believe in Christ Jesus.

Don't try to stop what the Holy Spirit is doing. Don't treat prophecies as if they weren't important. But test all prophecies. Hold on to what is good. Say no to every kind of evil.

God is the God who gives peace. May he make you holy through and through. May your whole spirit, soul and body be kept free from blame. May you be without blame from now until our Lord Jesus Christ comes. The God who has chosen you is faithful. He will do all these things.

May the grace of our Lord Jesus Christ be with you.

introduction to 2 Thessalonians

So that was Paul's first letter to the Thessalonians. But soon Paul had to write a second letter, because there was a nasty rumor going around that Paul was saying the "day of the Lord" had already come. (Can you guess who might have told Paul about this rumor? Here's a hint: This person helped Paul write his first letter to the Thessalonians. If you guessed Timothy, you're probably right!)

The "day of the Lord" is how the Bible talks about a time in the future when God will defeat his enemies and reward those who believe in him. If the rumor was true—and the day of the Lord was already here—then why were the Thessalonians still suffering? Why were their enemies still causing trouble for them? Wasn't God going to do something about it? Imagine how you'd feel if you were in their situation. Sad? Confused? Let down?

Paul gives the Thessalonians hope in this letter. He tells them that the day of the Lord hasn't arrived yet and promises that God will "pay back trouble" to those who cause trouble for believers.

Most of Paul's letter was written down by a scribe, which is a fancy name for a writer. But at the end of this letter, Paul writes a greeting in his own handwriting. Why do you think he does this? If he's trying to stop a false rumor about things he's been saying, then he needs to prove that this letter is from him, so the Thessalonians can trust what it says.

⌒∿∿∿⌒

I, Paul, am writing this letter. Silas and Timothy join me in writing.

We are sending this letter to you, the members of the church in Thessalonica. You belong to God our Father and the Lord Jesus Christ.

May God the Father and the Lord Jesus Christ give you grace and peace.

Brothers and sisters, we should always thank God for you. That is only right, because your faith is growing more and more. We also thank God that the love you all have for one another is increasing. So among God's churches we brag about the fact that you don't give up easily. We brag about your faith in all the suffering and testing you are going through.

All of this proves that when God judges, he is fair. So you will be considered worthy to enter God's kingdom. You are suffering for his kingdom. God is fair. He will pay back trouble to those who give you trouble. He will help you who are troubled. And he will also help us. All these things will happen when the Lord Jesus appears from heaven. He will come in blazing fire. He will come with his powerful angels. He will punish those who don't know God. He will punish those who don't obey the good news about our Lord Jesus. They will be destroyed forever. They will be shut out of heaven. They will never see the glory of the Lord's strength. All these things will happen when he comes. On that day his glory will be seen in his holy people. Everyone who has believed will be amazed when they see him. This includes you, because you believed the witness we gave you.

Keeping this in mind, we never stop praying for you. Our God has chosen you. We pray that he will make you worthy of his choice. We pray he will make every good thing you want to do come true. We pray that he will do this by his power. We pray that he will make perfect all that you have done by faith. We pray this so that the name of our Lord Jesus will receive glory through what you have done. We also pray that you will receive glory through what he has done. We pray all these things in keeping with the grace of our God and the Lord Jesus Christ.

Brothers and sisters, we want to ask you something. It has to do with the coming of our Lord Jesus Christ. It concerns the time when we will go to be with him. What if you receive a message that is supposed to have come from us? What if it says that the day of the Lord has already come? If it does, we ask you not to become easily upset or alarmed. Don't be upset whether that message is spoken or written or prophesied. Don't let anyone trick you in any way. That day will not come until people rise up against God. It will not come until the man of sin appears. He is a marked man. He is headed for ruin. He will oppose everything that is called God. He will oppose everything that is worshiped. He will give himself power over everything. He will set himself up in God's temple. He will announce that he himself is God.

Don't you remember? When I was with you, I used to tell you these things.

ↄᏦᎧ

Brothers and sisters, we should always thank God for you. The Lord loves you. That's because God chose you as the first to be saved. Salvation comes through the Holy Spirit's work. He makes people holy. It also comes through believing the truth. He chose you to be saved by accepting the good news that we preach. And you will share in the glory of our Lord Jesus Christ.

Brothers and sisters, remain strong in the faith. Hold on to what we taught you. We passed our teachings on to you by what we preached and wrote.

Our Lord Jesus Christ and God our Father loved us. By his grace God gave us comfort that will last forever. The hope he gave us is good. May our Lord Jesus Christ and God our Father comfort your hearts. May they make you strong in every good thing you do and say.

I, Paul, write this greeting in my own handwriting. That's how I prove that I am the author of all my letters. I always do it that way.

May the grace of our Lord Jesus Christ be with you all.

remember what you read

1. What is something you noticed for the first time?

_____

_____

_____

_____

2. What questions did you have?

_____

_____

_____

_____

3. Was there anything that bothered you?

_____

_____

_____

_____

4. What did you learn about loving God?

_____

_____

_____

_____

5. What did you learn about loving others?

_____

_____

_____

_____

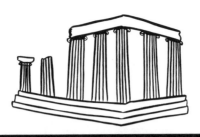

introduction to ı Corinthians, part ı

The apostle Paul traveled across the Roman Empire, telling people about Jesus. One of the places he visited was a very powerful and wealthy city called Corinth. Paul started a church there, and he stayed for about a year-and-a-half. But things took a turn for the worse after Paul left Corinth for Ephesus, a city across the sea about 250 miles away.

When a few believers from Corinth came to visit Paul, they brought alarming news. They also carried a letter from the church at Corinth, filled with lots of questions for Paul. We don't have this letter anymore, but we do have Paul's reply. It's found in the Bible, and it's called the book of 1 Corinthians.

The church in Corinth was tearing itself apart. People were fighting with each other over which leaders to follow. They were arguing over who had the most knowledge and thinking they were better than everyone else. Paul had to do something.

Today we'll read the first part of his letter to the believers in Corinth. As you do, pay attention to the advice he gives them. And ask yourself: what might Paul say to a group of Christians fighting with each other today?

I, Paul, am writing this letter. I have been chosen to be an apostle of Christ Jesus just as God planned. Our brother Sosthenes joins me in writing.

We are sending this letter to you, the members of God's church in Corinth. You have been made holy because you belong to Christ

Jesus. God has chosen you to be his holy people. He has done the same for all people everywhere who pray to our Lord Jesus Christ. Jesus is their Lord and ours.

May God our Father and the Lord Jesus Christ give you grace and peace.

I always thank my God for you. I thank him because of the grace he has given to you who belong to Christ Jesus. You have been blessed in every way because of him. You have been blessed in all your speech and knowledge. God has shown that what we have spoken to you about Christ is true. There is no gift of the Holy Spirit that you don't have. You are full of hope as you wait for our Lord Jesus Christ to come again. God will also keep you strong in faith to the very end. Then you will be without blame on the day our Lord Jesus Christ returns. God is faithful. He has chosen you to share life with his Son, Jesus Christ our Lord.

ᘓᘏᘏᘎ

Brothers and sisters, I make my appeal to you. I do this in the name of our Lord Jesus Christ. I ask that all of you agree with one another in what you say. I ask that you don't take sides. I ask that you are in complete agreement in all that you think. My brothers and sisters, I have been told you are arguing with one another. Some people from Chloe's house have told me this. Here is what I mean. One of you says, "I follow Paul." Another says, "I follow Apollos." Another says, "I follow Peter." And still another says, "I follow Christ."

Does Christ take sides? Did Paul die on the cross for you? Were you baptized in the name of Paul? I thank God that I didn't baptize any of you except Crispus and Gaius. No one can say that you were baptized in my name. It's true that I also baptized those who live in the house of Stephanas. Besides that, I don't remember if I baptized anyone else. Christ did not send me to baptize. He sent me to preach the good news. He commanded me not to preach with wisdom and fancy words. That would take all the power away from the cross of Christ.

The message of the cross seems foolish to those who are lost and dying. But it is God's power to us who are being saved. It is written,

"I will destroy the wisdom of those who are wise.
  I will do away with the cleverness of those who think they
    are so smart."

Where is the wise person? Where is the teacher of the law? Where are the great thinkers of our time? Hasn't God made the wisdom of the world foolish? God wisely planned that the world would not know him through its own wisdom. It pleased God to use the foolish things we preach to save those who believe. Jews require signs. Greeks look for wisdom. But we preach about Christ and his death on the cross. That is very hard for Jews to accept. And everyone else thinks it's foolish. But there are those God has chosen, both Jews and Greeks. To them Christ is God's power and God's wisdom. The foolish things of God are wiser than human wisdom. The weakness of God is stronger than human strength.

Brothers and sisters, think of what you were when God chose you. Not many of you were considered wise by human standards. Not many of you were powerful. Not many of you belonged to important families. But God chose the foolish things of the world to shame the wise. God chose the weak things of the world to shame the strong. God chose the things of this world that are common and looked down on. God chose things considered unimportant to do away with things considered important. So no one can boast to God. Because of what God has done, you belong to Christ Jesus. He has become God's wisdom for us. He makes us right with God. He makes us holy and sets us free. It is written, "The one who boasts should boast about what the Lord has done."

And this was the way it was with me, brothers and sisters. When I came to you, I didn't come with fancy words or human wisdom. I preached to you the truth about God's love. My goal while I was with you was to talk about only one thing. And that was Jesus Christ and his death on the cross. When I came to you, I was weak and very afraid and trembling all over. I didn't preach my message with clever and compelling words. Instead, my preaching showed the Holy Spirit's power. This was so that your faith would be based on God's power. Your faith would not be based on human wisdom.

The words we speak to those who have grown in the faith are wise. Our words are different from the wisdom of this world. Our words are different from those of the rulers of this world. These rulers are becoming less and less powerful. No, we announce God's wisdom. His wisdom is a mystery that has been hidden. But before time began, God planned that his wisdom would bring us heavenly glory. None of the rulers of this world understood God's wisdom. If they had, they would not have nailed the Lord of glory to the cross. It is written that

"no eye has seen,
    no ear has heard,
and no human mind has known."
    God has prepared these things for those who love him.

God has shown these things to us through his Spirit.

The Spirit understands all things. He understands even the deep things of God. Who can know the thoughts of another person? Only a person's own spirit can know them. In the same way, only the Spirit of God knows God's thoughts. What we have received is not the spirit of the world. We have received the Spirit who is from God. The Spirit helps us understand what God has freely given us. That is what we speak about. We don't use words taught to us by people. We use words taught to us by the Holy Spirit. We use the words taught by the Spirit to explain spiritual truths. The person without the Spirit doesn't accept the things that come from the Spirit of God. These things are foolish to them. They can't understand them. In fact, such things can't be understood without the Spirit's help. The person who has the Spirit can judge all things. But no human being can judge those who have the Spirit. It is written,

"Who can ever know what is in the Lord's mind?
    Can anyone ever teach him?"

But we have the mind of Christ.

Brothers and sisters, I couldn't speak to you as people who live by the Holy Spirit. I had to speak to you as people who were still following the ways of the world. You aren't growing as Christ wants you to. You are still like babies. The words I spoke to you were like milk, not like solid food. You weren't ready for solid food yet. And you still aren't ready for it. You are still following the ways of the world. Some of you are jealous. Some of you argue. So aren't you following the ways of the world? Aren't you acting like ordinary human beings? One of you says, "I follow Paul." Another says, "I follow Apollos." Aren't you acting like ordinary human beings?

After all, what is Apollos? And what is Paul? We are only people who serve. We helped you to believe. The Lord has given each of us our own work to do. I planted the seed. Apollos watered it. But God has been making it grow. So the one who plants is not important. The one who waters is not important. It is God who makes things grow. He is the important one. The one who plants and the one who waters have the same purpose. The Lord will give each of them a reward for their work. We work together to serve God. You are like God's field. You are like his building.

God has given me the grace to lay a foundation as a wise builder. Now someone else is building on it. But each one should build carefully. No one can lay any other foundation than what has already been laid. That foundation is Jesus Christ.

Don't you know that you yourselves are God's temple? Don't you know that God's Spirit lives among you? If anyone destroys God's temple, God will destroy that person. God's temple is holy. And you all together are that temple.

Don't fool yourselves. Suppose some of you think you are wise by the standards of the world. Then you should become "fools" so that you can become wise. The wisdom of this world is foolish in God's eyes. It is written, "God catches wise people in their own evil plans." It is also written, "The Lord knows that the thoughts of wise people don't amount to anything." So no more bragging about human leaders! All things are yours. That means Paul or Apollos or Peter or the world or life or death or the present or the future. All are yours. You are joined to Christ and belong to him. And Christ is joined to God.

So here is how you should think of us. We serve Christ. We are trusted with the mysteries God has shown us. Those who have been given a trust must prove that they are faithful. I care very little if I am judged by you or by any human court. I don't even judge myself. I don't feel I have done anything wrong. But that doesn't mean I'm not guilty. The Lord judges me. So don't judge anything before the appointed time. Wait until the Lord returns. He will bring to light what is hidden in the dark. He will show the real reasons why people do what they do. At that time each person will receive their praise from God.

Brothers and sisters, I have used myself and Apollos as examples to help you. You can learn from us the meaning of the saying, "Don't go beyond what is written." Then you won't be proud that you follow one of us instead of the other. Who makes you different from anyone else? What do you have that you did not receive? And if you did receive it, why do you brag as though you did not?

remember what you read

1. What is something you noticed for the first time?

_____

_____

_____

_____

2. What questions did you have?

_____

_____

_____

_____

3. Was there anything that bothered you?

_____

_____

_____

_____

4. What did you learn about loving God?

_____

_____

_____

_____

5. What did you learn about loving others?

_____

_____

_____

_____

1 CORINTHIANS, PART 2

introduction to 1 Corinthians, part 2

In the first part of his letter to the church in Corinth, Paul told believers there to stop fighting with each other. But that was only the beginning of their problems. The Corinthians had lots of questions for Paul.

They wanted to know if it was OK to eat food that had been dedicated to other gods. They wanted to know which gifts of the Holy Spirit were better than others. They were starting to ask if Jesus really rose from the dead or not.

Pay attention to how Paul answers each of these questions in the second part of his letter.

But be careful how you use your rights. Be sure you don't cause someone weaker than you to fall into sin.

I am free and don't belong to anyone. But I have made myself a slave to everyone. I do it to win as many as I can to Christ. I have become all things to all people. I have done this so that in all possible ways I might save some. I do all this because of the good news. And I want to share in its blessings.

So eat and drink and do everything else for the glory of God. Don't do anything that causes another person to trip and fall. It doesn't matter if that person is a Jew or a Greek or a member of God's church. Follow my example. I try to please everyone in every way. I'm not looking out for what is good for me. I'm looking out for the interests of others. I do it so that they might be saved.

I praise you for being faithful in remembering me. I also praise you for staying true to the teachings of the past. You have stayed true to them, just as I gave them to you. In the following matters, I don't praise you. Your meetings do more harm than good. First, here is what people are telling me. When you come together as a church, you take sides. And in some ways I believe it. Do you really think you need to take sides? You probably think God favors one side over the other! So when you come together, it is not the Lord's Supper you eat. As you eat, some of you go ahead and eat your own private meals. Because of this, one person stays hungry and another gets drunk. Don't you have homes to eat and drink in? You are shaming those in the church who have nothing. Do you think so little of God's church that you do this? What should I say to you? Should I praise you? Certainly not about the Lord's Supper!

I passed on to you what I received from the Lord. On the night the Lord Jesus was handed over to his enemies, he took bread. When he had given thanks, he broke it. He said, "This is my body. It is given for you. Every time you eat it, do it in memory of me." In the same way, after supper he took the cup. He said, "This cup is the new covenant in my blood. Every time you drink it, do it in memory of me." You eat the bread and drink the cup. When you do this, you are announcing the Lord's death until he comes again.

Eat the bread or drink the cup of the Lord in the right way. Don't do it in a way that isn't worthy of him.

My brothers and sisters, when you come together to eat, you should all eat together. Anyone who is hungry should eat something at home. Then when you come together, you will not be judged.

Brothers and sisters, I want you to know about the gifts of the Holy Spirit.

The Holy Spirit is given to each of us in a special way. That is for the good of all. To some people the Spirit gives a message of wisdom. To others the same Spirit gives a message of knowledge. To others the same Spirit gives faith. To others that one Spirit gives gifts of healing. To others he gives the power to do miracles. To others he gives the ability to prophesy. To others he gives the ability to tell the spirits apart. To others he gives the ability to speak in different kinds of languages they had not known before. And to still others he gives the ability to explain what was said in those languages. All the gifts are produced by one and the same Spirit. He gives gifts to each person, just as he decides.

There is one body, but it has many parts. But all its many parts make up one body. It is the same with Christ. We were all baptized by one Holy Spirit. And so we are formed into one body. It didn't matter whether we were Jews or Gentiles, slaves or free people. We were all given the same Spirit to drink. So the body is not made up of just one part. It has many parts.

Suppose the foot says, "I am not a hand. So I don't belong to the body." By saying this, it cannot stop being part of the body. And suppose the ear says, "I am not an eye. So I don't belong to the body." By saying this, it cannot stop being part of the body. If the whole body were an eye, how could it hear? If the whole body were an ear, how could it smell? God has placed each part in the body just as he wanted it to be. If all the parts were the same, how could there be a body? As it is, there are many parts. But there is only one body.

The eye can't say to the hand, "I don't need you!" The head can't say to the feet, "I don't need you!" In fact, it is just the opposite. The parts of the body that seem to be weaker are the ones we can't do without. The parts that we think are less important we treat with special honor. The private parts aren't shown. But they are treated with special care. The parts that can be shown don't need special care. But God has put together all the parts of the body. And he has given more honor to the parts that didn't have any. In that way, the parts of the body will not take sides. All of them will take care of one another. If one part suffers, every part suffers with it. If one part is honored, every part shares in its joy.

You are the body of Christ. Each one of you is a part of it.

But now I will show you the best way of all.

Suppose I speak in the languages of human beings or of angels. If I don't have love, I am only a loud gong or a noisy cymbal. Suppose I have the gift of prophecy. Suppose I can understand all the secret things of God and know everything about him. And suppose I have enough faith to move mountains. If I don't have love, I am nothing at all. Suppose I give everything I have to poor people. And suppose I give myself over to a difficult life so I can brag. If I don't have love, I get nothing at all.

Love is patient. Love is kind. It does not want what belongs to others. It does not brag. It is not proud. It does not dishonor other people. It does not look out for its own interests. It does not easily become angry. It does not keep track of other people's wrongs. Love is not happy with evil. But it is full of joy when the truth is spoken. It always protects. It always trusts. It always hopes. It never gives up.

Love never fails. But prophecy will pass away. Speaking in languages that had not been known before will end. And knowledge will pass away.

The three most important things to have are faith, hope and love. But the greatest of them is love.

ᘏᘏᘏ

Brothers and sisters, I want to remind you of the good news I preached to you. You received it and have put your faith in it. Because you believed the good news, you are saved. But you must hold firmly to the message I preached to you. If you don't, you have believed it for nothing.

What I received I passed on to you. And it is the most important of all. Here is what it is. Christ died for our sins, just as Scripture said he would. He was buried. He was raised from the dead on the third day, just as Scripture said he would be. He appeared to Peter. Then he appeared to the 12 apostles. After that, he appeared to more than 500 brothers and sisters at the same time. Most of them are still living. But some have died. He appeared to James. Then he appeared to all the apostles. Last of all, he also appeared to me. I was like someone who wasn't born at the right time.

We have preached that Christ has been raised from the dead. So how can some of you say that no one rises from the dead? If no one rises from the dead, then not even Christ has been raised. And if Christ has not been raised, what we preach doesn't mean anything. Your faith doesn't mean anything either. More than that, we would be lying about God.

But Christ really has been raised from the dead. He is the first of all those who will rise from the dead.

But someone will ask, "How are the dead raised? What kind of body will they have?" How foolish! What you plant doesn't come to life unless it dies. When you plant something, it isn't a completely grown plant that you put in the ground. You only plant a seed. Maybe it's wheat or something else. But God gives the seed a body just as he has planned. And to each kind of seed he gives its own body.

It will be like that with bodies that are raised from the dead. The body that is planted does not last forever. The body that is raised from the dead lasts forever. It is planted without honor. But it is raised in glory. It is planted in weakness. But it is raised in power. It is planted as an earthly body. But it is raised as a spiritual body.

Brothers and sisters, here is what I'm telling you. Bodies made of flesh and blood can't share in the kingdom of God. And what dies can't share in what never dies. Listen! I am telling you a mystery. We will not all die. But we will all be changed. That will happen in a flash, as quickly as you can wink an eye. It will happen at the blast of the last trumpet. Then the dead will be raised to live forever. And we will be changed. Our natural bodies don't last forever. They must be dressed with what does last forever. What dies must be dressed with what does not die. In fact, that is going to happen. What does not last will be dressed with what lasts forever. What dies will be dressed with what does not die. Then what is written will come true. It says, "Death has been swallowed up. It has lost the battle."

But let us give thanks to God! He gives us the victory because of what our Lord Jesus Christ has done.

My dear brothers and sisters, remain strong in the faith. Don't let anything move you. Always give yourselves completely to the work of the Lord. Because you belong to the Lord, you know that your work is not worthless.

Now I want to deal with the offering of money for the Lord's people. Do what I told the churches in Galatia to do. On the first day of every week, each of you should put some money away. The amount should be in keeping with how much money you make. Save the money so that you won't have to take up an offering when I come.

Be on your guard. Remain strong in the faith. Be brave. Be loving in everything you do.

May the grace of the Lord Jesus be with you.

remember what you read

1. What is something you noticed for the first time?

_____

_____

_____

_____

2. What questions did you have?

_____

_____

_____

_____

3. Was there anything that bothered you?

_____

_____

_____

_____

4. What did you learn about loving God?

_____

_____

_____

_____

5. What did you learn about loving others?

_____

_____

_____

_____

2 CORINTHIANS

introduction to 2 Corinthians

The story of Paul and the church he started in Corinth is like one big roller coaster ride: full of ups and downs. In his first letter to the Corinthians, Paul urged them to stop fighting with each other. And he had to deal with a lot of other problems, too.

Paul wrote another letter, not long after sending his first one. By this time, the Corinthians were starting to listen. Most of them were trying to do the right thing. Paul wrote this letter, known as 2 Corinthians, to encourage them. He wanted them to know that all was forgiven—that he still loved them. He also wanted to let them know that he was sending his friend Titus to help take up an offering for the poor.

There were still problems, of course. Some people still questioned Paul's authority. In response, Paul decides to do a little bragging. But see if you notice anything unusual about his bragging.

ᘯᘯᘯ

I, Paul, am writing this letter. I am an apostle of Christ Jesus just as God planned. Timothy our brother joins me in writing.

We are sending this letter to you, the members of God's church in Corinth. It is also for all God's holy people everywhere in Achaia.

May God our Father and the Lord Jesus Christ give you grace and peace.

Give praise to the God and Father of our Lord Jesus Christ! He is the Father who gives tender love. All comfort comes from him. He comforts us in all our troubles. Now we can comfort others when they are in trouble. Our hope for you remains firm. We know that you suffer just as we do. In the same way, God comforts you just as he comforts us.

Since we have that kind of hope, we are very bold.

So because of God's mercy, we have work to do. He has given it to us. And we don't give up. Instead, we have given up doing secret and shameful things. We don't twist God's word. In fact, we do just the opposite. We present the truth plainly. The message we preach is not about ourselves. Our message is about Jesus Christ. We say that he is Lord. And we say that we serve you because of Jesus.

We are pushed hard from all sides. But we are not beaten down. We are bewildered. But that doesn't make us lose hope. Others make us suffer. But God does not desert us. We are knocked down. But we are not knocked out.

We know that God raised the Lord Jesus from the dead. And he will also raise us up with Jesus. And he will present both you and us to himself. All this is for your benefit. God's grace is reaching more and more people. So they will become more and more thankful. They will give glory to God.

Christ died for everyone. He died so that those who live should not live for themselves anymore. They should live for Christ. He died for them and was raised again.

So from now on we don't look at anyone the way the world does. At one time we looked at Christ in that way. But we don't anymore. When anyone lives in Christ, the new creation has come. The old is gone! The new is here! All this is from God. He brought us back to himself through Christ's death on the cross. And he has given us the task of bringing others back to him through Christ. God was bringing the world back to himself through Christ. He did not hold people's sins against them. God has trusted us with the message that people may be brought back to him. So we are Christ's official messengers. It is as if God were making his appeal through us. Here is what Christ wants us to beg you to do. Come back to God! Christ didn't have any sin. But God made him become sin for us. So we can be made right with God because of what Christ has done for us.

⚘

When we came to Macedonia, we weren't able to rest. We were attacked no matter where we went. We had battles on the outside and fears on the inside. But God comforts those who are sad. He comforted us when Titus came. We were comforted not only when he came but also by the comfort you had given him. He told us how much you longed for me. He told us about your deep sadness and concern for me. That made my joy greater than ever.

⚘

Brothers and sisters, we want you to know about the grace that God has given to the churches in Macedonia. They have suffered a great deal. But in their suffering, their joy was more than full. Even though they were very poor, they gave very freely. I tell you that they gave as much as they could. In fact, they gave even more than they could. Completely on their own, they begged us for the chance to share in serving the Lord's people in that way. They did more than we expected. First they gave themselves to the Lord. Then they gave themselves to us because that was what God wanted. Titus had already started collecting money from you. So we asked him to help you finish making your kind gift. You do well in everything else. You do well in faith and in speaking. You do well in knowledge and in complete commitment. And you do well in the love we have helped to start in you. So make sure that you also do well in the grace of giving to others.

God put into the heart of Titus the same concern I have for you. Thanks should be given to God for this. Titus welcomed our appeal. He is also excited about coming to you. It was his own idea. Along with Titus, we are sending another brother.

Titus is my helper. He and I work together among you. Our brothers are messengers from the churches. They honor Christ. So show them that you really love them. Show them why we are proud of you. Then the churches can see it.

They will finish the plans for the large gift you had promised. Then it will be ready as a gift freely given. It will not be given by force.

Here is something to remember. The one who plants only a little will gather only a little. And the one who plants a lot will gather a lot. Each of you should give what you have decided in your heart to give. You shouldn't give if you don't want to. You shouldn't give because you are forced to. God loves a cheerful giver. Your gifts meet the needs of the Lord's people. And that's not all. Your gifts also cause many people to thank God. You have shown yourselves to be worthy by what you have given. So other people will praise God because you obey him. That proves that you really believe the good news about Christ. They will also praise God because you share freely with them and with everyone else. Their hearts will be filled with love for you when they pray for you. God has given you grace that is better than anything. Let us give thanks to God for his gift. It is so great that no one can tell how wonderful it really is!

Please don't make me be as bold as I expect to be toward some people.

Do I brag too much about the authority the Lord gave me? If I do, it's because I want to build you up, not tear you down. And I'm not ashamed of that kind of bragging. Don't think that I'm trying to scare you with my letters. Some say, "His letters sound important. They are powerful. But in person he doesn't seem like much. And what he says doesn't amount to anything." People like that have a lot to learn. What I say in my letters when I'm away from you, I will do in my actions when I'm with you.

Whatever anyone else dares to brag about, I also dare to brag about. I'm speaking like a fool! Are they Hebrews? So am I. Do they belong to the people of Israel? So do I. Are they Abraham's children? So am I. Are they serving Christ? I am serving him even more. I'm out of my mind to talk like this! I have worked much harder. I have been in prison more often. I have suffered terrible beatings. Again and again I almost died. Five times the Jews gave me 39 strokes with a whip. Three times I was beaten with sticks. Once they tried to kill me by throwing stones at me. Three times

I was shipwrecked. I spent a night and a day in the open sea. I have had to keep on the move. I have been in danger from rivers. I have been in danger from robbers. I have been in danger from my fellow Jews and in danger from Gentiles. I have been in danger in the city, in the country, and at sea. I have been in danger from people who pretended they were believers. I have worked very hard. Often I have gone without sleep. I have been hungry and thirsty. Often I have gone without food. I have been cold and naked. Besides everything else, every day I am concerned about all the churches. It is a very heavy load. If anyone is weak, I feel weak. If anyone is led into sin, I burn on the inside.

So I am very happy to brag about how weak I am. Then Christ's power can rest on me. Because of how I suffered for Christ, I'm glad that I am weak. I am glad in hard times. I am glad when people say mean things about me. I am glad when things are difficult. And I am glad when people make me suffer. When I am weak, I am strong.

⟳⟳⟳

Now I am ready to visit you for the third time. I won't cause you any expense. I don't want what you have. What I really want is you. After all, children shouldn't have to save up for their parents. Parents should save up for their children. So I will be very happy to spend everything I have for you. I will even spend myself. If I love you more, will you love me less?

All this time, have you been thinking that I've been speaking up for myself? No, I've been speaking with God as my witness. I've been speaking like a believer in Christ. Dear friends, everything I do is to help you become stronger. I'm afraid that when I come I won't find you as I want you to be. I'm afraid that you won't find me as you want me to be. I'm afraid there will be arguing, jealousy and fits of anger. I'm afraid each of you will focus only on getting ahead. Then you will tell lies about each other. You will talk about each other. I'm afraid you will be proud and cause trouble. I'm afraid that when I come again my God will put me to shame in front of you. Then I will be sad about many who sinned earlier and have not turned away from it.

Take a good look at yourselves to see if you are really believers. Test yourselves. Don't you realize that Christ Jesus is in you? Unless, of course, you fail the test! I hope you will discover that I haven't failed the test. I pray to God that you won't do anything wrong. I don't pray so that people will see that I have passed the test. Instead, I pray this so that you will do what is right, even if it seems I have failed. I can't do anything to stop the truth. I can only work for the truth. I'm glad when I am weak but you are strong. I pray that there will be no more problems among you. That's why I write these things before I come to you. Then when I do come, I won't have to be hard on you when I use my authority. The Lord gave me the authority to build you up. He didn't give it to me to tear you down.

Finally, brothers and sisters, be joyful! Work to make things right with one another. Help one another and agree with one another. Live in peace. And the God who gives love and peace will be with you.

remember what you read

1. What is something you noticed for the first time?

_____

_____

_____

_____

2. What questions did you have?

_____

_____

_____

_____

3. Was there anything that bothered you?

_____

_____

_____

_____

4. What did you learn about loving God?

_____

_____

_____

_____

5. What did you learn about loving others?

_____

_____

_____

_____

introduction to Galatians

The apostle Paul made several trips through a province called Galatia. Usually, he traveled through Galatia on his way somewhere else. But once, he had to stop there because he got sick. Some nice people in Galatia helped Paul get better—and he helped them become followers of Jesus.

Later, some other people came to Galatia. They said you had to follow their rules in order to be saved. According to them, you had to do as they said if you wanted God to love you.

The worst part is, people in Galatia were starting to believe it! So Paul wrote a letter to set the record straight. He said we don't have to follow a bunch of rules or rituals to be saved. We just have to put our faith in Jesus. When we do, he sets us free so we can love and serve others. He gives us the Holy Spirit's power so we can live as he wants us to.

Paul had some hard words for the people in Galatia, but that's because he loved them and didn't want them to miss the good news that Jesus had for them. According to Paul, there's only one thing you need if you want to be saved. Do you know what that is?

I, Paul, am writing this letter. I am an apostle. People have not sent me. No human authority has sent me. I have been sent by Jesus Christ and by God the Father. God raised Jesus from the dead. All the brothers and sisters who are with me join me in writing.

We are sending this letter to you, the members of the churches in Galatia.

May God our Father and the Lord Jesus Christ give you grace and peace. Jesus gave his life for our sins. He set us free from this evil world. That was what our God and Father wanted. Give glory to God for ever and ever. Amen.

☙

I am amazed. You are so quickly deserting the one who chose you. He chose you to live in the grace that Christ has provided. You are turning to a different "good news." What you are accepting is really not the good news at all. It seems that some people have gotten you all mixed up. They are trying to twist the good news about Christ. But suppose even we should preach a different "good news." Suppose even an angel from heaven should preach it. Suppose it is different from the good news we gave you. Then let anyone who does that be cursed by God. I have already said it. Now I will say it again. Suppose someone preaches a "good news" that is different from what you accepted. That person should be cursed by God.

Brothers and sisters, here is what I want you to know. The good news I preached does not come from human beings. No one gave it to me. No one taught it to me. Instead, I received it from Jesus Christ. He showed it to me.

☙

You foolish people of Galatia! Who has put you under an evil spell? When I preached, I clearly showed you that Jesus Christ had been nailed to the cross. I would like to learn just one thing from you. Did you receive the Holy Spirit by obeying the law? Or did you receive the Spirit by believing what you heard? Are you so foolish? You began by the Holy Spirit. Are you now trying to finish God's work in you by your own strength? Have you experienced so much for nothing? And was it really for nothing? So I ask you again, how does God give you his Spirit? How does he work miracles among you? Is it by doing what the law says? Or is it by believing what you have heard? In the same way, Abraham "believed God. God was pleased with Abraham because he believed. So his faith made him right with God."

So you see, those who have faith are children of Abraham. Long ago, Scripture knew that God would make the Gentiles right with himself. He would do this by their faith in him. He announced the good news ahead of time to Abraham. God said, "All nations will be blessed because of you." So those who depend on faith are blessed along with Abraham. He was the man of faith.

All who depend on obeying the law are under a curse. It is written, "May everyone who doesn't continue to do everything written in the Book of the Law be under God's curse." We know that no one who depends on the law is made right with God. This is because "the one who is right with God will live by faith." The law is not based on faith. In fact, it is just the opposite. It teaches that "the person who does these things will live by them." Christ set us free from the curse of the law. He did it by becoming a curse for us. It is written, "Everyone who is hung on a pole is under God's curse." Christ Jesus set us free so that the blessing given to Abraham would come to the Gentiles through Christ. He did it so that we might receive the promise of the Holy Spirit. The promised Spirit comes by believing in Christ.

Before faith in Christ came, we were guarded by the law. We were locked up until this faith was made known. So the law was put in charge of us until Christ came. He came so that we might be made right with God by believing in Christ. But now faith in Christ has come. So the law is no longer in charge of us.

So in Christ Jesus you are all children of God by believing in Christ. This is because all of you who were baptized into Christ have put on Christ. You have put him on as if he were your clothes. There is no Jew or Gentile. There is no slave or free person. There is no male or female. That's because you are all one in Christ Jesus. You who belong to Christ are Abraham's seed. So you will receive what God has promised.

⁓ഏഏ⁓

My brothers and sisters, you were chosen to be free. But don't use your freedom as an excuse to live under the power of sin.

Instead, serve one another in love. The whole law is fulfilled by obeying this one command. "Love your neighbor as you love yourself." If you say or do things that harm one another, watch out! You could end up destroying one another.

So I say, live by the Holy Spirit's power. Then you will not do what your desires controlled by sin want you to do.

But the fruit the Holy Spirit produces is love, joy and peace. It is being patient, kind and good. It is being faithful and gentle and having control of oneself. There is no law against things of that kind. Those who belong to Christ Jesus have nailed their sinful desires to his cross. They don't want these things anymore. Since we live by the Spirit, let us keep in step with the Spirit. Let us not become proud. Let us not make each other angry. Let us not want what belongs to others.

Each person should test their own actions. Then they can take pride in themselves. They won't be comparing themselves to someone else. Each person should carry their own load.

Let us not become tired of doing good. At the right time we will gather a crop if we don't give up. So when we can do good to everyone, let us do it. Let's try even harder to do good to the family of believers.

Brothers and sisters, may the grace of our Lord Jesus Christ be with your spirit. Amen.

remember what you read

1. What is something you noticed for the first time?

_____

_____

_____

_____

2. What questions did you have?

_____

_____

_____

_____

3. Was there anything that bothered you?

_____

_____

_____

_____

4. What did you learn about loving God?

_____

_____

_____

_____

5. What did you learn about loving others?

_____

_____

_____

_____

ROMANS, PART 1

introduction to Romans, part 1

Thanks to Paul and his friends, the good news about Jesus had been shared with people all over the eastern part of the Roman Empire. But Paul wasn't going to stop there. He wanted to go to other places where people still hadn't heard the news.

So he started planning a trip. This time, he was going where no other Christian had gone yet. He was going to visit the western half of the Roman Empire.

Right in between east and west was the capital city: Rome. Paul knew there some Christians there who could help him on his journey. So wrote them a letter and gave it to a friend named Pheobe, a church leader who was traveling to Rome.

After introducing himself, Paul gets right down to business: he wants them to know that Jesus is for everyone. The good news isn't just for Jews like Paul; it's also for people who aren't Jewish. Both Jews and non-Jews have a place in God's family.

Everyone has sinned, Paul says. No one can save themselves. We all need Jesus. That's why Paul wants to go where no other Christian has gone. That's why he plans to visit the western half of the Roman Empire. And that's why he's hoping the church in Rome will support him on his journey.

As you read, notice how Paul uses the story of a man named Abraham to make his point. You may recognize this name. Abraham was the father of the Jewish people. And according to Paul, even Abraham needed to be saved by faith.

I, Paul, am writing this letter. I serve Christ Jesus. I have been appointed to be an apostle. God set me apart to tell others his good news. He made us apostles to the Gentiles. We must invite all of them to obey God by trusting in Jesus. We do this to bring glory to him. You also are among those Gentiles who are appointed to belong to Jesus Christ.

I am sending this letter to all of you in Rome. You are loved by God and appointed to be his holy people.

May God our Father and the Lord Jesus Christ give you grace and peace.

~✺~

First, I thank my God through Jesus Christ for all of you. People all over the world are talking about your faith. I serve God with my whole heart. I preach the good news about his Son. God knows that I always remember you in my prayers. I pray that now at last it may be God's plan to open the way for me to visit you.

I long to see you. I want to make you strong by giving you a gift from the Holy Spirit. I want us to encourage one another in the faith we share. Brothers and sisters, I want you to know that I planned many times to visit you. But until now I have been kept from coming. My work has produced results among the other Gentiles. In the same way, I want to see results among you.

I have a duty both to Greeks and to non-Greeks. I have a duty both to wise people and to foolish people. So I really want to preach the good news also to you who live in Rome.

I want to preach it because I'm not ashamed of the good news. It is God's power to save everyone who believes. It is meant first for the Jews. It is meant also for the Gentiles. The good news shows God's power to make people right with himself. God's power to be made right with him is given to the person who has faith. It happens by faith from beginning to end. It is written, "The one who is right with God will live by faith."

~✺~

Ever since the world was created it has been possible to see the qualities of God that are not seen. I'm talking about his eternal power and about the fact that he is God. Those things can be seen in what he has made. So people have no excuse for what they do. They knew God. But they didn't honor him as God. They didn't thank him. Their thinking became worthless. Their foolish hearts became dark. They claimed to be wise. But they made fools of themselves. They would rather have statues of gods than the glorious God who lives forever. Their statues of gods are made to look like people, birds, animals and reptiles.

So God let them go. He allowed them to do what their sinful hearts wanted to. They made one another's bodies impure by what they did.

What should we say then? Do we Jews have any advantage? Not at all! We have already claimed that Jews and Gentiles are sinners. Everyone is under the power of sin. It is written,

"No one is right with God, no one at all.
    No one understands.
    No one trusts in God.
All of them have turned away.

But now God has shown us his saving power without the help of the law. But the Law and the Prophets tell us about this. We are made right with God by putting our faith in Jesus Christ. This happens to all who believe. It is no different for the Jews than for the Gentiles. Everyone has sinned. No one measures up to God's glory. The free gift of God's grace makes us right with him. Christ Jesus paid the price to set us free. God gave Christ as a sacrifice to pay for sins through the spilling of his blood. So God forgives the sins of those who have faith. God did all this to prove that he does what is right. He is a God of mercy. So he did not punish for their sins the people who lived before Jesus lived. God did all this to prove in our own time that he does what is right. He also makes right with himself those who believe in Jesus.

So who can brag? No one! Are people saved by the law that requires them to obey? Not at all! They are saved because of the law that requires faith. We firmly believe that a person is made right with God because of their faith. They are not saved by obeying the law. Or is God the God of Jews only? Isn't he also the God of Gentiles? Yes, he is their God too. There is only one God. When those who are circumcised believe in him, he makes them right with himself. Suppose those who are not circumcised believe in him. Then God also will make them right with himself. Does faith make the law useless? Not at all! We agree with the law.

Abraham and his family received a promise. God promised that Abraham would receive the world. It would not come to him because he obeyed the law. It would come because of his faith, which made him right with God.

The promise is based on God's grace. The promise comes by faith. All of Abraham's children will certainly receive the promise. And it is not only for those who are ruled by the law. Those who have the same faith that Abraham had are also included. He is the father of us all. It is written, "I have made you a father of many nations." God considers Abraham to be our father. The God that Abraham believed in gives life to the dead. Abraham's God also creates things that did not exist before.

When there was no reason for hope, Abraham believed because he had hope. He became the father of many nations, exactly as God had promised. God said, "That is how many children you will have." Abraham did not become weak in his faith. He accepted the fact that he was past the time when he could have children. At that time Abraham was about 100 years old. He also realized that Sarah was too old to have children. But Abraham kept believing in God's promise. He became strong in his faith. He gave glory to God. He was absolutely sure that God had the power to do what he had promised. That's why "God accepted Abraham because he believed. So his faith made him right with God." The words "God accepted Abraham's faith" were written not only for Abraham. They were written also for us. We believe in the God who raised Jesus our Lord from the dead. So God will accept our faith and make us right with himself. Jesus was handed over to die for our sins. He was raised to life in order to make us right with God.

We have been made right with God because of our faith. Now we have peace with him because of our Lord Jesus Christ. Through faith in Jesus we have received God's grace. In that grace we stand. We are full of joy because we expect to share in God's glory. And that's not all. We are full of joy even when we suffer. We know that our suffering gives us the strength to go on. The strength to go on produces character. Character produces hope. And hope will never bring us shame. That's because God's love has been poured into our hearts. This happened through the Holy Spirit, who has been given to us.

At just the right time Christ died for ungodly people. He died for us when we had no power of our own. It is unusual for anyone to die for a godly person. Maybe someone would be willing to die for a good person. But here is how God has shown his love for us. While we were still sinners, Christ died for us.

The blood of Christ has made us right with God. So we are even more sure that Jesus will save us from God's anger. Once we were God's enemies. But we have been brought back to him because his Son has died for us. Now that God has brought us back, we are even more secure. We know that we will be saved because Christ lives. And that is not all. We are full of joy in God because of our Lord Jesus Christ. Because of him, God has brought us back to himself.

◌◌◌

We know that in all things God works for the good of those who love him. He appointed them to be saved in keeping with his purpose. God planned that those he had chosen would become like his Son. In that way, Christ will be the first and most honored among many brothers and sisters. And those God has planned for, he has also appointed to be saved. Those he has appointed, he has made right with himself. To those he has made right with himself, he has given his glory.

What should we say then? Since God is on our side, who can be against us? God did not spare his own Son. He gave him up for us all. Then won't he also freely give us everything else? Who can bring any charge against God's chosen ones? God makes us right with himself. Then who can sentence us to death? No one. Christ Jesus is at the right hand of God and is also praying for us. He died. More than that, he was raised to life. Who can separate us from Christ's love? Can trouble or hard times or harm or hunger? Can nakedness or danger or war? No! In all these things we are more than winners! We owe it all to Christ, who has loved us. I am absolutely sure that not even death or life can separate us from God's love. Not even angels or demons, the present or the future, or any powers can separate us. Not even the highest places or the lowest, or anything else in all creation can separate us. Nothing at all can ever separate us from God's love. That's because of what Christ Jesus our Lord has done.

remember what you read

1. What is something you noticed for the first time?

_____

_____

_____

_____

2. What questions did you have?

_____

_____

_____

_____

3. Was there anything that bothered you?

_____

_____

_____

_____

4. What did you learn about loving God?

_____

_____

_____

_____

5. What did you learn about loving others?

_____

_____

_____

_____

ROMANS, PART 2

introduction to Romans, part 2

In the first part of his letter to believers in Rome, Paul wrote that Jesus is for everyone. It didn't matter to God whether a person was Jewish, like Paul, or non-Jewish, like many of Paul's friends.

But there was a problem. Long before Jesus came, God choose the people of Israel—that is, the Jews—to be his special people. He made a covenant with them—a binding promise that he would be their God, and they would be his people.

So if God was now reaching out to everyone, did that mean he had forgotten about Israel? Had he had broken his special promise with them?

See if you notice how Paul answers this very difficult question. Here's a clue: the answer has something to do with all of us being a part of one big family.

Speaking of families, Paul closes his letter with some advice about how we can live together and serve each other as followers of Jesus.

❧❧❧

My heart is full of sorrow. My sadness never ends. I am so concerned about my people, who are members of my own race. They are the people of Israel. They have been adopted as God's children. God's glory belongs to them. So do the covenants. They received the law. They were taught to worship in the temple. They were given the promises. The founders of our nation belong to them. The Messiah comes from their family line. He is God over all. May he always be praised! Amen.

I do not mean that God's word has failed. Not everyone in the family line of Israel really belongs to Israel. Not everyone in Abraham's family line is really his child. In other words, God's children are not just in the family line of Abraham. Instead, they are the children God promised to him. They are the ones considered to be Abraham's children.

What should we say then? Is God unfair? Not at all! He said to Moses,

"I will have mercy on whom I have mercy.
I will show love to those I love."

So it doesn't depend on what people want or what they do. It depends on God's mercy.

One of you will say to me, "Then why does God still blame us? Who can oppose what he wants to do?" But you are a mere human being. So who are you to talk back to God? Scripture says, "Can what is made say to the one who made it, 'Why did you make me like this?'" Isn't the potter free to make different kinds of pots out of the same lump of clay? Some are for special purposes. Others are for ordinary use.

What if God chose to show his great anger? What if he chose to make his power known? But he put up with the people he was angry with. They were made to be destroyed. What if he put up with them to show the riches of his glory to other people? Those other people are the ones he shows his mercy to. He made them to receive his glory. We are those people. He has chosen us. We do not come only from the Jewish race. Many of us are not Jews. God says in Hosea,

"I will call those who are not my people 'my people.'
I will call the one who is not my loved one 'my loved one.'"

What should we say then? Gentiles did not look for a way to be right with God. But they found it by having faith. The people of Israel tried to obey the law to make themselves right with God. But they didn't reach their goal of being right with God. Why not? Because they tried to do it without faith. They tried to be right with

God by what they did. They tripped over the stone that causes people to trip and fall.

Brothers and sisters, with all my heart I long for the people of Israel to be saved. I pray to God for them. I can tell you for certain that they really want to serve God. But how they are trying to do it is not based on knowledge. They didn't know that God's power makes people right with himself. They tried to get right with God in their own way. They didn't do it in God's way. Christ has fulfilled everything the law was meant to do. So now everyone who believes can be right with God.

There is no difference between those who are Jews and those who are not. The same Lord is Lord of all. He richly blesses everyone who calls on him. Scripture says, "Everyone who calls on the name of the Lord will be saved."

So here is what I ask. Did God turn his back on his people? Not at all! I myself belong to Israel.

Again, here is what I ask. The Israelites didn't trip and fall once and for all time, did they? Not at all! Because Israel sinned, the Gentiles can be saved. That will make Israel jealous of them. Israel's sin brought riches to the world. Their loss brings riches to the Gentiles. So then what greater riches will come when all Israel turns to God!

I am talking to you who are not Jews. I am the apostle to the Gentiles. So I take pride in the work I do for God and others. I hope somehow to stir up my own people to want what you have. Perhaps I can save some of them.

God does not take back his gifts. He does not change his mind about those he has chosen. At one time you did not obey God. But now you have received mercy because Israel did not obey. In the same way, Israel has not been obeying God. But now they receive mercy because of God's mercy to you. God has found everyone guilty of not obeying him. So now he can have mercy on everyone.

How very rich are God's wisdom and knowledge!
How he judges is more than we can understand!
The way he deals with people is more than we can know!

"Who can ever know what the Lord is thinking?
Or who can ever give him advice?"
"Has anyone ever given anything to God,
so that God has to pay them back?"
All things come from him.
All things are directed by him.
All things are for his praise.
May God be given the glory forever! Amen.

~~~

Brothers and sisters, God has shown you his mercy. So I am asking you to offer up your bodies to him while you are still alive. Your bodies are a holy sacrifice that is pleasing to God. When you offer your bodies to God, you are worshiping him in the right way. Don't live the way this world lives. Let your way of thinking be completely changed. Then you will be able to test what God wants for you. And you will agree that what he wants is right. His plan is good and pleasing and perfect.

God's grace has been given to me. So here is what I say to every one of you. Don't think of yourself more highly than you should. Be reasonable when you think about yourself.

Love must be honest and true. Hate what is evil. Hold on to what is good. Love one another deeply. Honor others more than yourselves. Stay excited about your faith as you serve the Lord. When you hope, be joyful. When you suffer, be patient. When you pray, be faithful. Share with the Lord's people who are in need. Welcome others into your homes.

Bless those who hurt you. Bless them, and do not curse them. Be joyful with those who are joyful. Be sad with those who are sad. Agree with one another. Don't be proud. Be willing to be a friend of people who aren't considered important. Don't think that you are better than others.

Don't pay back evil with evil. Be careful to do what everyone thinks is right. If possible, live in peace with everyone. Do that as much as you can.

Don't let evil overcome you. Overcome evil by doing good.

Here are some commandments to think about. "Do not commit adultery." "Do not commit murder." "Do not steal." "Do not want what belongs to others." These and all other commands are included in one command. Here's what it is. "Love your neighbor as you love yourself." Love does not harm its neighbor. So love does everything the law requires.

When you do these things, keep in mind the times we are living in. The hour has already come for you to wake up from your sleep. The full effects of our salvation are closer now than when we first believed in Christ. The dark night of evil is nearly over. The day of Christ's return is almost here. So let us get rid of the works of darkness that harm us. Let us do the works of light that protect us.

Accept the person whose faith is weak. Don't argue with them where you have differences of opinion.

We who have strong faith should help the weak with their problems. We should not please only ourselves. Each of us should please our neighbors. Let us do what is good for them in order to build them up. Everything written in the past was written to teach us. The Scriptures give us strength to go on. They encourage us and give us hope.

Our God is a God who strengthens and encourages you. May he give you the same attitude toward one another that Christ Jesus had. Then you can give glory to God with one mind and voice. He is the God and Father of our Lord Jesus Christ.

Christ has accepted you. So accept one another in order to bring praise to God.

May the God who gives hope fill you with great joy. May you have perfect peace as you trust in him. May the power of the Holy Spirit fill you with hope.

༄༅༅

I am warning you, brothers and sisters, to watch out for those who try to keep you from staying together. They want to trip you up. They teach you things opposite to what you have learned. Stay away from them. People like that are not serving Christ our Lord. They are serving only themselves. With smooth talk and with

words they don't mean they fool people who don't know any better. Everyone has heard that you obey God. So you have filled me
with joy. I want you to be wise about what is good. And I want you
to have nothing to do with what is evil.

The God who gives peace will soon crush Satan under your feet.

May the grace of our Lord Jesus be with you.

remember what you read

1. What is something you noticed for the first time?

_____

_____

_____

_____

2. What questions did you have?

_____

_____

_____

_____

3. Was there anything that bothered you?

_____

_____

_____

_____

4. What did you learn about loving God?

_____

_____

_____

_____

5. What did you learn about loving others?

_____

_____

_____

_____

introduction to Colossians

Paul's life was quite the adventure. If you remember from the book of Acts (a few readings back), Paul was planning a trip to Rome, the most powerful city in the world at the time. But first, he had to make a stop in Jerusalem to drop off a collection for the poor. Sound familiar? Well, that's because this was the same collection he mentioned in his letters to the church in Corinth.

Unfortunately, Paul had plenty of enemies waiting for him in Jerusalem. When he arrived, a citywide riot broke out. Paul was put in jail; but because he was a Roman citizen, he had the right to appeal his case to the emperor. And so he was taken to Rome, where he spent the next two years under house arrest, waiting for his case to be heard.

Paul wasn't about to stop working just because he was under guard. He continued writing letters, encouraging and instructing churches across the Roman Empire. One of these letters was written to the church in Colosse.

Paul had never been to Colosse, but one of his friends, Epaphras, grew up there and told Paul all about the believers there. Paul wrote to encourage them in their faith, but also to warn them not to listen to anyone who said they had to follow certain rules or rituals to be saved. When you have Jesus, Paul said, you've got it all!

As you read Paul's letter, you might hear some familiar—and unfamiliar—names. See if you recognize any of the people Paul mentions near the end of his letter.

There's at least one name you haven't heard yet: Onesimus. Remember this name. It's going to come up very soon in another one of Paul's letters.

༄༅

I, Paul, am writing this letter. I am an apostle of Christ Jesus just as God planned. Our brother Timothy joins me in writing.

We are sending this letter to you, our brothers and sisters in Colossae. You belong to Christ. You are holy and faithful.

May God our Father give you grace and peace.

We always thank God, the Father of our Lord Jesus Christ, when we pray for you. We thank him because we have heard about your faith in Christ Jesus. We have also heard that you love all God's people. Your faith and love are based on the hope you have. What you hope for is stored up for you in heaven. You have already heard about it. You were told about it when the true message was given to you. I'm talking about the good news that has come to you. In the same way, the good news is bearing fruit. It is bearing fruit and growing all over the world. It has been doing that among you since the day you heard it. That is when you really understood God's grace. You learned the good news from Epaphras. He is dear to us. He serves Christ together with us. He faithfully works for Christ and for us among you. He also told us about your love that comes from the Holy Spirit.

That's why we have not stopped praying for you. We have been praying for you since the day we heard about you. We keep asking God to fill you with the knowledge of what he wants. We pray he will give you the wisdom and understanding that the Spirit gives. Then you will be able to lead a life that is worthy of the Lord. We pray that you will please him in every way. So we want you to bear fruit in every good thing you do. We pray that you will grow to know God better. We want you to be very strong, in keeping with his glorious power. We want you to be patient. We pray that you will never give up. We want you to give thanks with joy to the Father. He has made you fit to have what he will give to all his holy people. You will all receive a share in the kingdom of light. He has saved us from the kingdom of darkness. He has brought us into the kingdom of the Son he loves. Because of what the Son has done, we have been set free. Because of him, all our sins have been forgiven.

The Son is the exact likeness of God, who can't be seen. The Son is first, and he is over all creation. All things were created in him. He created everything in heaven and on earth. He created everything that can be seen and everything that can't be seen. He created kings, powers, rulers and authorities. All things have been created by him and for him. Before anything was created, he was already there. He holds everything together. And he is the head of the body, which is the church. He is the beginning. He is the first to be raised from the dead. That happened so that he would be far above everything. God was pleased to have his whole nature living in Christ. God was pleased to bring all things back to himself. That's because of what Christ has done. These things include everything on earth and in heaven. God made peace through Christ's blood, by his death on the cross.

At one time you were separated from God. You were enemies in your minds because of your evil ways. But because Christ died, God has brought you back to himself. Christ's death has made you holy in God's sight. So now you don't have any flaw. You are free from blame. But you must keep your faith steady and firm. You must not move away from the hope the good news holds out to you. This is the good news that you heard. It has been preached to every creature under heaven. I, Paul, now serve the good news.

I am happy because of what I am suffering for you. My suffering joins with and continues the sufferings of Christ. I suffer for his body, which is the church. I serve the church. God appointed me to bring the complete word of God to you. That word contains the mystery that has been hidden for many ages. But now it has been made known to the Lord's people. God has chosen to make known to them the glorious riches of that mystery. He has made it known among the Gentiles. And here is what it is. Christ is in you. He is your hope of glory.

Christ is the one we preach about. With all the wisdom we have, we warn and teach everyone. When we bring them to God, we want them to be like Christ. We want them to be grown up as people who belong to Christ. That's what I'm working for. I work hard with all the strength of Christ. His strength works powerfully in me.

I want you to know how hard I am working for you. But I don't want anyone to fool you with words that only sound good.

You received Christ Jesus as Lord. So keep on living your lives in him. Have your roots in him. Build yourselves up in him. Grow strong in what you believe, just as you were taught. Be more thankful than ever before.

Make sure no one controls you. They will try to control you by using false reasoning that has no meaning. Their ideas depend on human teachings. They also depend on the basic spiritual powers of this world. They don't depend on Christ.

God's whole nature is living in Christ in human form. Because you belong to Christ, you have been made complete. He is the ruler over every power and authority.

At one time you were dead in your sins. But God gave you new life together with Christ. He forgave us all our sins.

So don't let anyone judge you because of what you eat or drink. Don't let anyone judge you about holy days. I'm talking about special feasts and New Moons and Sabbath days. They are only a shadow of the things to come. But what is real is found in Christ. Some people enjoy pretending they aren't proud. They worship angels. But don't let people like that judge you. These people tell you every little thing about what they have seen. They are proud of their useless ideas. That's because their minds are not guided by the Holy Spirit. They aren't connected anymore to the head, who is Christ. But the whole body grows from the head. The muscles and tendons hold the body together. And God causes it to grow.

You have been raised up with Christ. So think about things that are in heaven. That is where Christ is. He is sitting at God's right hand. Think about things that are in heaven. Don't think about things that are only on earth. You died. Now your life is hidden with Christ in God. Christ is your life. When he appears again, you also will appear with him in heaven's glory.

So put to death anything that comes from sinful desires. Get rid of sexual sins and impure acts. Don't let your feelings get out of control. Remove from your life all evil desires. Stop always wanting more and more. You must get rid of anger, rage, hate and lies. Let no dirty words come out of your mouths. Don't lie to one another. You have gotten rid of your old way of life and its habits. You have started living a new life. Your knowledge of how that life should have the Creator's likeness is being made new. Here there is no Gentile or Jew. There is no difference between those who are circumcised and those who are not. There is no rude outsider, or even a Scythian. There is no slave or free person. But Christ is everything. And he is in everything.

You are God's chosen people. You are holy and dearly loved. So put on tender mercy and kindness as if they were your clothes. Don't be proud. Be gentle and patient. Put up with one another. Forgive one another if you are holding something against someone. Forgive, just as the Lord forgave you. And over all these good things put on love. Love holds them all together perfectly as if they were one.

Let the peace that Christ gives rule in your hearts. As parts of one body, you were appointed to live in peace. And be thankful. Let the message about Christ live among you like a rich treasure. Teach and correct one another wisely. Teach one another by singing psalms and hymns and songs from the Spirit. Sing to God with thanks in your hearts. Do everything you say or do in the name of the Lord Jesus. Always give thanks to God the Father through Christ.

Give a lot of time and effort to prayer. Always be watchful and thankful. Pray for us too. Pray that God will give us an opportunity to preach our message. Then we can preach the mystery of Christ. Because I preached it, I am being held by chains. Pray that I will preach it clearly, as I should. Be wise in the way you act toward outsiders. Make the most of every opportunity. Let the words you speak always be full of grace. Learn how to make your words what people want to hear. Then you will know how to answer everyone.

Tychicus will tell you all the news about me. He is a dear brother. He is a faithful worker. He serves the Lord together with us. I am sending him to you for one reason. I want you to know what is happening here. I want him to encourage you and make your hearts strong. He is coming with Onesimus, our faithful and dear brother. He is one of you. They will tell you everything that is happening here.

Aristarchus is in prison with me. He sends you his greetings. So does Mark, the cousin of Barnabas. You have been given directions about him. If he comes to you, welcome him.

Our dear friend Luke, the doctor, sends greetings. So does Demas.

Give my greetings to the brothers and sisters in Laodicea. Also give my greetings to Nympha and the church that meets in her house.

After this letter has been read to you, send it on. Be sure that it is also read to the church in Laodicea. And be sure that you read the letter from Laodicea.

I, Paul, am writing this greeting with my own hand. Remember that I am being held by chains. May grace be with you.

remember what you read

1. What is something you noticed for the first time?

_____

_____

_____

_____

2. What questions did you have?

_____

_____

_____

_____

3. Was there anything that bothered you?

_____

_____

_____

_____

4. What did you learn about loving God?

_____

_____

_____

_____

5. What did you learn about loving others?

_____

_____

_____

_____

introduction to Ephesians

When Paul wrote his last letter—the one we know as Colossians—he was a prisoner in Rome, awaiting trial before the emperor. He asked his friends Tychicus and Onesimus to deliver the letter, along with at least two others he had written.

One of these is the letter known as Ephesians. We don't know for sure who it was written to, but we do know they were Gentiles—non-Jewish people who had put their faith in Jesus.

Paul tells them they are "God's people." It doesn't matter one bit whether they are Jewish or not. God is creating a new worldwide family, where everyone is welcome, regardless of the color of their skin, their race, or their background.

And because they're part of a new family, Paul encourages them to live like one. Pay attention to the practical advice he gives. And see if you notice what powerful "weapons" he tells his readers to use in the fight against sin.

∞

I, Paul, am writing this letter. I am an apostle of Christ Jesus just as God planned.

May God our Father and the Lord Jesus Christ give you grace and peace.

Give praise to the God and Father of our Lord Jesus Christ. He has blessed us with every spiritual blessing. Those blessings come from the heavenly world. They belong to us because we belong to Christ. God chose us to belong to Christ before the world was created. He chose us to be holy and without blame in his eyes. He loved us. So he decided long ago to adopt us. He adopted us as his children with all the rights children have. He did it because of what Jesus Christ has done. It pleased God to do it. All those things bring praise to his glorious grace. God freely gave us his grace because of the One he loves. We have been set free because of what Christ has done. Because he bled and died our sins have been forgiven. We have been set free because God's grace is so rich. He poured his grace on us. By giving us great wisdom and understanding, he showed us the mystery of his plan. It was in keeping with what he wanted to do. It was what he had planned through Christ. It will all come about when history has been completed. God will then bring together all things in heaven and on earth under Christ.

I have heard about your faith in the Lord Jesus. I have also heard about your love for all God's people. That is why I have not stopped thanking God for you. I always remember you in my prayers.

You were living in your sins and lawless ways. But in fact you were dead. You used to live as sinners when you followed the ways of this world. You served the one who rules over the spiritual forces of evil. He is the spirit who is now at work in those who don't obey God. At one time we all lived among them. Our desires were controlled by sin. We tried to satisfy what they wanted us to do. We followed our desires and thoughts. God was angry with us like he was with everyone else. That's because of the kind of people we all were. But God loves us deeply. He is full of mercy. So he gave us new life because of what Christ has done. He gave us life even when we were dead in sin. God's grace has saved you. God raised us up with Christ. Your salvation doesn't come from anything you do. It is God's gift. It is not based on anything you have done. No one can brag about earning it. We are God's creation. He created us to belong to Christ Jesus. Now we can do good works. Long ago God prepared these works for us to do.

~~~

You who are not Jews by birth, here is what I want you to remember. Before you believed in Christ, you were separated from him.

You were not considered to be citizens of Israel. You were not included in what the covenants promised. You were without hope and without God in the world. At one time you were far away from God. But now you belong to Christ Jesus. He spilled his blood for you. This has brought you near to God.

Christ himself is our peace. He has made Jews and Gentiles into one group of people. He has destroyed the hatred that was like a wall between us. Through his body on the cross, Christ set aside the law with all its commands and rules. He planned to create one new people out of Jews and Gentiles. He wanted to make peace between them.

So you are no longer outsiders and strangers. You are citizens together with God's people. You are also members of God's family.

◌ᕙᕗ◌

I am a prisoner because of the Lord. So I am asking you to live a life worthy of what God chose you for. Don't be proud at all. Be completely gentle. Be patient. Put up with one another in love. The Holy Spirit makes you one in every way. So try your best to remain as one. Let peace keep you together. There is one body and one Spirit. You were appointed to one hope when you were chosen. There is one Lord, one faith and one baptism. There is one God and Father of all. He is over everything. He is through everything. He is in everything.

So each of you must get rid of your lying. Speak the truth to your neighbor. We are all parts of one body.

Get rid of all hard feelings, anger and rage. Stop all fighting and lying. Don't have anything to do with any kind of hatred. Be kind and tender to one another. Forgive one another, just as God forgave you because of what Christ has done.

You are the children that God dearly loves. So follow his example. Lead a life of love, just as Christ did. He loved us. He gave himself up for us.

Speak to one another with psalms, hymns and songs from the Spirit. Sing and make music from your heart to the Lord. Always give thanks to God the Father for everything. Give thanks to him in the name of our Lord Jesus Christ.

Follow the lead of one another because of your respect for Christ. Wives, follow the lead of your own husbands as you follow the Lord.

Husbands, love your wives. Love them just as Christ loved the church.

Children, obey your parents as believers in the Lord. Obey them because it's the right thing to do.

Fathers, don't make your children angry. Instead, instruct them and teach them the ways of the Lord as you raise them.

Slaves, obey your masters here on earth. Respect them and honor them with a heart that is true.

Masters, treat your slaves in the same way. When you warn them, don't be too hard on them. You know that the God who is their Master and yours is in heaven. And he treats everyone the same.

Finally, let the Lord make you strong. Depend on his mighty power. Put on all of God's armor. Then you can remain strong against the devil's evil plans.Put the belt of truth around your waist. Put the armor of godliness on your chest. Wear on your feet what will prepare you to tell the good news of peace. Also, pick up the shield of faith. With it you can put out all the flaming arrows of the evil one. Put on the helmet of salvation. And take the sword of the Holy Spirit. The sword is God's word.

At all times, pray by the power of the Spirit. Pray all kinds of prayers. Be watchful, so that you can pray. Always keep on praying for all the Lord's people. Pray also for me. Pray that whenever I speak, the right words will be given to me. Then I can be bold as I tell the mystery of the good news. Because of the good news, I am being held by chains as the Lord's messenger. So pray that I will be bold as I preach the good news. That's what I should do.

Tychicus is a dear brother. He is faithful in serving the Lord. He will tell you everything about me. Then you will know how I am and what I am doing. That's why I am sending him to you. I want you to know how we are. And I want him to encourage you.

May grace be given to everyone who loves our Lord Jesus Christ with a love that will never die.

introduction to Philemon

It seems hard to imagine, but slavery—one person owning another— was all too common in Paul's day. If you were a slave, you were someone else's property. You didn't have any rights. And if you ran away, you could be hunted down and punished by brutal slave-catchers.

One of Paul's friends was a runaway slave named Onesimus. You might recognize this name from Paul's letter to the Colossians. Onesimus belonged to a man named Philemon, a member of the church in Colosse. But Onesimus had run away.

He wound up in Rome, where he met Paul and become a follower of Jesus. Now, Paul was sending Onesimus back to Colosse.

For Onesimus, going back meant risking everything. He was putting himself at the mercy of his master, Philemon.

But he wouldn't be going back empty-handed. Paul wrote this letter, urging Philemon to welcome Onesimus not as a slave, but as his equal.

Why? Because, as Paul once wrote in another letter, in Christ there is no slave or free person. We are all one. We are all members of the same family.

We don't know for sure what happened to Onesimus. What do you think? Did Philemon take Paul's advice and welcome his old slave as a brother?

I, Paul, am writing this letter. I am a prisoner because of Christ Jesus. Our brother Timothy joins me in writing.

Philemon, we are sending you this letter. You are our dear friend.

May God our Father and the Lord Jesus Christ give you grace and peace.

I always thank my God when I remember you in my prayers. That's because I hear about your love for all God's people. Your love has given me great joy. It has encouraged me. My brother, you have renewed the hearts of the Lord's people.

Because of the authority Christ has given me, I could be bold. I could order you to do what you should do anyway. But we love each other. And I would rather appeal to you on the basis of that love. I, Paul, am an old man. I am now also a prisoner because of Christ Jesus. I am an old man, and I'm in prison. This is how I make my appeal to you for my son Onesimus. He became a son to me while I was being held in chains. Before that, he was useless to you. But now he has become useful to you and to me.

I'm sending Onesimus back to you. All my love for him goes with him. I'm being held in chains because of the good news. So I would have liked to keep Onesimus with me. And he could take your place in helping me. But I didn't want to do anything unless you agreed. Any favor you do must be done because you want to do it, not because you have to. Onesimus was separated from you for a little while. Maybe that was so you could have him back forever. You could have him back not as a slave. Instead, he would be better than a slave. He would be a dear brother. He is very dear to me but even more dear to you. He is dear to you not only as another human being. He is also dear to you as a brother in the Lord.

Do you think of me as a believer who works together with you? Then welcome Onesimus as you would welcome me. Has he done anything wrong to you? Does he owe you anything? Then charge it to me. I'll pay it back. I, Paul, am writing this with my own hand. I won't even mention that you owe me your life. I'm sure you will obey. So I'm writing to you. I know you will do even more than I ask.

There is one more thing. Have a guest room ready for me. I hope I can return to all of you in answer to your prayers.

Epaphras sends you greetings. Together with me, he is a prisoner because of Christ Jesus.

May the grace of the Lord Jesus Christ be with your spirit.

remember what you read

1. What is something you noticed for the first time?

_____

_____

_____

_____

2. What questions did you have?

_____

_____

_____

_____

3. Was there anything that bothered you?

_____

_____

_____

_____

4. What did you learn about loving God?

_____

_____

_____

_____

5. What did you learn about loving others?

_____

_____

_____

_____

PHILIPPIANS, 1 TIMOTHY

introduction to Philippians

Imagine you've been arrested for telling people about Jesus. You're taken to a strange city, far from home. You're about to be put on trial, and you don't know whether you're going to live or die.

How would you feel? Nervous? Scared? What about joyful?

It's not exactly the first thing that comes to mind, is it? But "joyful" is how Paul describes himself in his letter to the Philippians. At the time, Paul was being "held by chains," awaiting trial in Rome. He didn't know whether he'd be set free or sentenced to die.

Years earlier, Paul had started a church in the city of Philippi, about 600 miles from Rome. The believers there heard that Paul had been arrested and sent one of their members to help take care of him.

The letter you're about to read, Philippians, is basically a thank-you note. Paul tells the church in Philippi how grateful he is for their support. He also encourages them to stand together, because they, like him, are suffering hard times.

As you read, count how many times Paul talks about having "joy." And ask yourself: how can you have joy even when times are tough?

∽∾∽

We, Paul and Timothy, are writing this letter. We serve Christ Jesus.

We are sending this letter to you, all God's holy people in Philippi.

May God our Father and the Lord Jesus Christ give you grace and peace.

I thank my God every time I remember you. In all my prayers for all of you, I always pray with joy. I am happy because you have joined me in spreading the good news.

God began a good work in you. And I am sure that he will carry it on until it is completed. That will be on the day Christ Jesus returns.

It is right for me to feel this way about all of you. I love you with all my heart. I may be held by chains, or I may be standing up for the truth of the good news. Either way, all of you share in God's grace together with me.

I pray that your love will grow more and more. And let it be based on knowledge and understanding. Then you will be able to know what is best. Then you will be pure and without blame for the day that Christ returns.

⁂

Brothers and sisters, here is what I want you to know. What has happened to me has actually helped to spread the good news. One thing has become clear. I am being held by chains because I am a witness for Christ. And because I am a prisoner, most of the believers have become bolder in the Lord. They now dare even more to preach the good news without fear.

Here is what he has given you to do for Christ. You must not only believe in him. You must also suffer for him. You are going through the same struggle you saw me go through. As you have heard, I am still struggling.

⁂

So does belonging to Christ help you in any way? Does his love comfort you at all? Do you share anything in common because of the Holy Spirit? Has Christ ever been gentle and loving toward you? If any of these things has happened to you, then agree with one another. Have the same love. Be one in spirit and in the way you think and act. By doing this, you will make my joy complete. Don't do anything only to get ahead. Don't do it because you are proud. Instead, be humble. Value others more than yourselves.

None of you should look out just for your own good. Each of you should also look out for the good of others.

As you deal with one another, you should think and act as Jesus did.

In his very nature he was God.
Jesus was equal with God. But Jesus didn't take advantage
    of that fact.
Instead, he made himself nothing.
He did this by taking on the nature of a servant.
He was made just like human beings.
He appeared as a man.
He was humble and obeyed God completely.
He did this even though it led to his death.
    Even worse, he died on a cross!

So God lifted him up to the highest place.
God gave him the name that is above every name.
When the name of Jesus is spoken, everyone will kneel down
    to worship him.
Everyone in heaven and on earth and under the earth will
    kneel down to worship him.
Everyone's mouth will say that Jesus Christ is Lord.
And God the Father will receive the glory.

Further, my brothers and sisters, be joyful because you belong to the Lord!

I want to know Christ better. Yes, I want to know the power that raised him from the dead. I want to join him in his sufferings. I want to become like him by sharing in his death. Then by God's grace I will rise from the dead.

Brothers and sisters, I don't consider that I have taken hold of it yet. But here is the one thing I do. I forget what is behind me. I push hard toward what is ahead of me. I push myself forward toward the goal to win the prize. God has appointed me to win it. The heavenly prize is Christ Jesus himself.

I have learned the secret of being content no matter what happens. I am content whether I am well fed or hungry. I am content whether I have more than enough or not enough. I can do all this by the power of Christ. He gives me strength.

But it was good of you to share in my troubles. And you believers at Philippi know what happened when I left Macedonia. Not one church helped me in the matter of giving and receiving. You were the only one that did. And you did it more than once. My God will meet all your needs. He will meet them in keeping with his wonderful riches. These riches come to you because you belong to Christ Jesus.

Give glory to our God and Father for ever and ever. Amen.

introduction to 1 Timothy

After being held prisoner for two years in Rome, Paul was set free.

Now, if Paul were like most people, he would take it easy for a while. Keep quiet and stay out of trouble. But Paul had work to do, and he wasn't about to let a little thing like prison get in the way.

One of the churches Paul had started was in trouble. The church in Ephesus was drifting away from the truth. Their leaders were making people follow a bunch of religious rituals instead of trusting Jesus to save them. And they were allowing all kinds of sinful behavior.

Paul told his friend Timothy (you might remember him from the book of Acts) to stay in Ephesus and try to bring order to the church. In this letter, Paul gives Timothy advice for choosing good leaders who will stay true to Jesus. He also gives Timothy some instructions to share with the whole church.

Timothy was a young man when he led the church at Ephesus. So he might've worried that people wouldn't listen to him. Paul has some important encouragement for him; see if you notice what it is.

Timothy, I am sending you this letter. You are my true son in the faith.

May God the Father and Christ Jesus our Lord give you grace, mercy and peace.

Timothy, stay there in Ephesus. I want you to command certain people not to teach things that aren't true. Love is the purpose of my command. Love comes from a pure heart. It comes from a good sense of what is right and wrong. It comes from faith that is honest and true.

∽∽∽

I am thankful to Christ Jesus our Lord. He has given me strength. I thank him that he considered me faithful. I used to speak evil things against Jesus. I tried to hurt his followers. I really pushed them around. But God showed me mercy anyway.

Here is a saying that you can trust. It should be accepted completely. Christ Jesus came into the world to save sinners. And I am the worst sinner of all. But for that very reason, God showed me mercy.

∽∽∽

My son Timothy, I am giving you this command. It is in keeping with the prophecies once made about you. By remembering them, you can fight the battle well. Then you will hold on to faith.

First, I want you to pray for all people. Ask God to help and bless them. Give thanks for them. Pray for kings. Pray for everyone who is in authority. Pray that we can live peaceful and quiet lives. And pray that we will be godly and holy. This is good, and it pleases God our Savior. He wants all people to be saved. He wants them to come to know the truth. There is only one God. And there is only one go-between for God and human beings. He is the man Christ Jesus. He gave himself to pay for the sins of all people.

∽∽∽

Here is a saying you can trust. If anyone wants to be a leader in the church, they want to do a good work for God and people. A leader must be free from blame. He must be faithful to his wife. In anything he does, he must not go too far. He must control himself. He must be worthy of respect. He must welcome people into his home. He must be able to teach. He must not get drunk. He must not push people around. He must be gentle. He must not be a person who likes to argue. He must not love money.

〜〜〜

We have put our hope in the living God. He is the Savior of all people. Most of all, he is the Savior of those who believe.

Command and teach these things. Don't let anyone look down on you because you are young. Set an example for the believers in what you say and in how you live. Also set an example in how you love and in what you believe. Show the believers how to be pure. Until I come, spend your time reading Scripture out loud to one another. Spend your time preaching and teaching. Don't fail to use the gift the Holy Spirit gave you.

Be careful of how you live and what you believe. Never give up. Then you will save yourself and those who hear you.

You gain a lot when you live a godly life. But you must be happy with what you have. We didn't bring anything into the world. We can't take anything out of it. If we have food and clothing, we will be happy with that. Love for money causes all kinds of evil. Some people want to get rich. They have wandered away from the faith. They have wounded themselves with many sorrows.

But you are a man of God. Run away from all these things. Try hard to do what is right and godly. Have faith, love and gentleness. Hold on to what you believe. Fight the good fight along with all other believers. Take hold of eternal life.

Command the rich to do what is good. Tell them to be rich in doing good things. They must give freely. They must be willing to share. Timothy, guard what God has trusted you with.

May God's grace be with you all.

remember what you read

1. What is something you noticed for the first time?

_____

_____

_____

_____

2. What questions did you have?

_____

_____

_____

_____

3. Was there anything that bothered you?

_____

_____

_____

_____

4. What did you learn about loving God?

_____

_____

_____

_____

5. What did you learn about loving others?

_____

_____

_____

_____

introduction to Titus

After spending two years as a prisoner in Rome, Paul had his work cut out for him. There were big problems in Ephesus. In our last reading, Paul gave advice to his friend Timothy on how to lead the troubled church there.

A similar story was unfolding on the island of Crete. Much like Ephesus, the church on Crete was being taken over by people who believed you had to follow all sorts of rituals to get right with God. They were turning people away from faith in Jesus.

Paul sent another coworker, a man named Titus, to help the church on Crete.

As you read, see if you notice anything familiar about this letter. Does it remind you of Paul's first letter to Timothy? If so, that's because Paul gives Titus a lot of the same advice he shared with Timothy.

෨෨

I, Paul, am writing this letter. I serve God, and I am an apostle of Jesus Christ.

Titus, I am sending you this letter. You are my true son in the faith we share.

May God the Father and Christ Jesus our Savior give you grace and peace.

I left you on the island of Crete. I did this because there were some things that hadn't been finished. I wanted you to put them in order. I also wanted you to appoint elders in every town. I told you how to do it. An elder must be without blame. He must be faithful to his wife. His children must be believers. They must not give anyone a reason to say that they are wild and don't obey. A church leader takes care of God's family. That's why he must be without blame. He must not look after only his own interests. He must not get angry easily. He must not get drunk. He must not push people around. He must not try to get money by cheating people. Instead, a church leader must welcome people into his home. He must love what is good. He must control his mind and feelings. He must do what is right. He must be holy. He must control the desires of his body. The message as it has been taught can be trusted. He must hold firmly to it. Then he will be able to use true teaching to comfort others and build them up. He will be able to prove that people who oppose it are wrong.

Many people refuse to obey God. All they do is talk about things that mean nothing. They try to fool others. No one does these things more than the circumcision group. They must be stopped. They are making trouble for entire families. They do this by teaching things they shouldn't. They do these things to cheat people. They claim to know God. But their actions show they don't know him. They aren't fit to do anything good.

✿✿✿

No one can question the truth. So teach what is true. Then those who oppose you will be ashamed. That's because they will have nothing bad to say about us.

God's grace has now appeared. By his grace, God offers to save all people. His grace teaches us to say no to godless ways and sinful desires. We must control ourselves. We must do what is right. We must lead godly lives in today's world. That's how we should live as we wait for the blessed hope God has given us. We are waiting for Jesus Christ to appear in his glory. He is our great God and Savior.

These are the things you should teach. Encourage people and give them hope. Correct them with full authority. Don't let anyone look down on you.

Remind God's people to obey rulers and authorities. Remind them to be ready to do what is good. Tell them not to speak evil things against anyone. Remind them to live in peace. They must consider the needs of others. They must always be gentle toward everyone.

I will send Artemas or Tychicus to you. Then do your best to come to me at Nicopolis. I've decided to spend the winter there.

Everyone who is with me sends you greetings.
Greet those who love us in the faith.

May God's grace be with you all.

introduction to 2 Timothy

Things did not go well in Ephesus. Paul hoped that Timothy would be able to stop those leaders who were drawing people away from Jesus, but things only got worse. They refused to listen, and Timothy was discouraged.

Even worse, Paul had been arrested again. This time, he had little reason to hope he would get out alive. So he wrote Timothy one last time.

The letter you're about to read contains the final written words of Paul, the man who did more than anyone else to spread the good news about Jesus in the early days of the church.

Even though he's facing his own death, Paul uses most of his letter to encourage Timothy. Paul had come to think Timothy of as his own son. "Be strong," he urges. "Don't give up!"

Even at the end of his life, Paul had no regrets. He had fought the food fight. He'd finished the race. And even though things hadn't gone well in Ephesus, Paul had planted seeds of faith all over the Roman Empire. His legacy lives on to this day.

᷍ᩡᨆᨆᨆᩡ

I, Paul, am writing this letter. I am an apostle of Christ Jesus just as God planned.

Timothy, I am sending you this letter. You are my dear son.

May God the Father and Christ Jesus our Lord give you grace, mercy and peace.

I remember your tears. I long to see you so that I can be filled with joy. I remember your honest and true faith. It was alive first in your grandmother Lois and in your mother Eunice. And I am certain that it is now alive in you also.

This is why I remind you to help God's gift grow, just as a small spark grows into a fire. God gave us his Spirit. And the Spirit doesn't make us weak and fearful. Instead, the Spirit gives us power and love. He helps us control ourselves. So don't be ashamed of the message about our Lord. And don't be ashamed of me, his prisoner. Instead, join with me as I suffer for the good news. God's power will help us do that. God has saved us. He has chosen us to live a holy life. It wasn't because of anything we have done. It was because of his own purpose and grace. Through Christ Jesus, God gave us this grace even before time began. It has now been made known through the coming of our Savior, Christ Jesus. He has broken the power of death. Because of the good news, he has brought life out into the light. That life never dies.

My son, be strong in the grace that is yours in Christ Jesus. You have heard me teach in front of many witnesses. Pass on to people you can trust the things you've heard me say. Then they will be able to teach others also. Like a good soldier of Christ Jesus, join with me in suffering.

Remember Jesus Christ. He came from David's family line. He was raised from the dead. That is my good news. I am suffering for it. I have even been put in chains like someone who has committed a crime. But God's word is not held back by chains.

Here is a saying you can trust.

If we died with him,
    we will also live with him.
If we don't give up,
    we will also rule with him.

If we say we don't know him,
he will also say he doesn't know us.
Even if we are not faithful,
he remains faithful.
He must be true to himself.

Run away from the evil things that young people long for. Try hard to do what is right. Have faith, love and peace. Do these things together with those who call on the Lord from a pure heart. Don't have anything to do with arguing. It is dumb and foolish. You know it only leads to fights. Anyone who serves the Lord must not be hard to get along with. Instead, they must be kind to everyone. They must be able to teach. The one who serves must not hold anything against anyone. They must gently teach those who are against them. Maybe God will give a change of heart to those who are against you. That will lead them to know the truth. Maybe they will come to their senses. Maybe they will escape the devil's trap.

I give you a command in the sight of God and Christ Jesus. Preach the word. Be ready to serve God in good times and bad. Correct people's mistakes. Warn them. Encourage them with words of hope. Be very patient as you do these things. Teach them carefully. The time will come when people won't put up with true teaching. Instead, they will try to satisfy their own desires. They will gather a large number of teachers around them. The teachers will say what the people want to hear. But I want you to keep your head no matter what happens. Don't give up when times are hard. Work to spread the good news. Do everything God has given you to do.

I am already being poured out like a drink offering. The time when I will leave is near. I have fought the good fight. I have finished the race. I have kept the faith. Now there is a crown waiting for me. It is given to those who are right with God. The Lord, who judges fairly, will give it to me on the day he returns. He will not give it only to me. He will also give it to all those who are longing for him to return.

Do your best to come to me quickly. Get Mark and bring him with you.

The Lord will save me from every evil attack. He will bring me safely to his heavenly kingdom. Give him glory for ever and ever. Amen.

May the Lord be with your spirit. May God's grace be with you all.

remember what you read

1. What is something you noticed for the first time?

_____

_____

_____

_____

2. What questions did you have?

_____

_____

_____

_____

3. Was there anything that bothered you?

_____

_____

_____

_____

4. What did you learn about loving God?

_____

_____

_____

_____

5. What did you learn about loving others?

_____

_____

_____

_____

MATTHEW, PART I

introduction to Matthew, part I

The Bible includes not one but four books about the life of Jesus. Each book tells basically the same story, but each writer has a unique viewpoint.

Take Luke, for example. We've already heard his story. He wrote to show how Jesus came for everyone, including non-Jews.

But there's more to the story. You see, Jesus was also the rightful king of the Jews. Many years before he was born, God promised a savior who would come and rescue the Jews from all their troubles.

The book of Matthew tells the story of Jesus from this viewpoint. It shows how Jesus is that person: the savior and king of Israel.

If you know any Old Testament stories, you may notice something familiar about Matthew. For example, remember the story of Moses? How his family hid him from the angry king when Moses was just a baby? Well guess what? Something similar happens to Jesus in Matthew's story. See if you can tell what.

Or how about the time the Jews wandered in the desert and were tested for 40 years? Jesus has a similar "desert experience" in Matthew, which you'll hear more about in today's reading.

So why all the similarities to the Old Testament? Because Matthew is showing how Jesus fulfills everything in the Old Testament—how he is everything God promised long ago.

This is how the birth of Jesus the Messiah came about. His mother Mary and Joseph had promised to get married. But before they started to live together, it became clear that she was going to have a baby. She became pregnant by the power of the Holy Spirit. Her husband Joseph was faithful to the law. But he did not want to put her to shame in public. So he planned to divorce her quietly.

But as Joseph was thinking about this, an angel of the Lord appeared to him in a dream. The angel said, "Joseph, son of David, don't be afraid to take Mary home as your wife. The baby inside her is from the Holy Spirit. She is going to have a son. You must give him the name Jesus. That's because he will save his people from their sins."

All this took place to bring about what the Lord had said would happen. He had said through the prophet, "The virgin is going to have a baby. She will give birth to a son. And he will be called Immanuel." The name Immanuel means "God with us."

Jesus was born in Bethlehem in Judea. This happened while Herod was king of Judea. After Jesus' birth, Wise Men from the east came to Jerusalem. They asked, "Where is the child who has been born to be king of the Jews? We saw his star when it rose. Now we have come to worship him."

Then Herod secretly called for the Wise Men. He found out from them exactly when the star had appeared. He sent them to Bethlehem. He said, "Go and search carefully for the child. As soon as you find him, report it to me. Then I can go and worship him too."

After the Wise Men had listened to the king, they went on their way. The star they had seen when it rose went ahead of them. It finally stopped over the place where the child was. When they saw the star, they were filled with joy. The Wise Men went to the house. There they saw the child with his mother Mary. They bowed down and worshiped him. But God warned them in a dream not to go back to Herod. So they returned to their country on a different road.

When the Wise Men had left, Joseph had a dream. In the dream an angel of the Lord appeared to Joseph. "Get up!" the angel said. "Take the child and his mother and escape to Egypt. Stay there until I tell you to come back. Herod is going to search for the child. He wants to kill him."

So Joseph got up. During the night, he left for Egypt with the child and his mother Mary. Herod realized that the Wise Men had tricked him. So he became very angry. He gave orders about Bethlehem and the area around it. He ordered all the boys two years old and under to be killed.

After Herod died, Joseph had a dream while he was still in Egypt. In the dream an angel of the Lord appeared to him. The angel said, "Get up! Take the child and his mother. Go to the land of Israel. The people who were trying to kill the child are dead."

So Joseph got up. He took the child and his mother Mary back to the land of Israel. There he lived in a town called Nazareth.

In those days John the Baptist came and preached in the Desert of Judea. He said, "Turn away from your sins! The kingdom of heaven has come near." John is the one Isaiah the prophet had spoken about. He had said,

"A messenger is calling out in the desert,
'Prepare the way for the Lord.
    Make straight paths for him.'"

John's clothes were made out of camel's hair. He had a leather belt around his waist. His food was locusts and wild honey. People went out to him from Jerusalem and all Judea. They also came from the whole area around the Jordan River. When they confessed their sins, John baptized them in the Jordan.

Jesus came from Galilee to the Jordan River. He wanted to be baptized by John. But John tried to stop him. So he told Jesus, "I need to be baptized by you. So why do you come to me?"

Jesus replied, "Let it be this way for now. It is right for us to do this. It carries out God's holy plan." Then John agreed.

As soon as Jesus was baptized, he came up out of the water. At that moment heaven was opened. Jesus saw the Spirit of God coming down on him like a dove. A voice from heaven said, "This is my Son, and I love him. I am very pleased with him."

∽◌◌◌◌◌

The Holy Spirit led Jesus into the desert. There the devil tempted him. After 40 days and 40 nights of going without eating, Jesus was hungry. The tempter came to him. He said, "If you are the Son of God, tell these stones to become bread."

Jesus answered, "It is written, 'Man must not live only on bread. He must also live on every word that comes from the mouth of God.'"

Then the devil took Jesus to the holy city. He had him stand on the highest point of the temple. "If you are the Son of God," he said, "throw yourself down. It is written,

"'The Lord will command his angels to take good care of you.
They will lift you up in their hands.
Then you won't trip over a stone.'"

Jesus answered him, "It is also written, 'Do not test the Lord your God.'"

Finally, the devil took Jesus to a very high mountain. He showed him all the kingdoms of the world and their glory. "If you bow down and worship me," he said, "I will give you all this."

Jesus said to him, "Get away from me, Satan! It is written, 'Worship the Lord your God. He is the only one you should serve.'"

Then the devil left Jesus. Angels came and took care of him.

∽◌◌◌◌◌

One day Jesus was walking beside the Sea of Galilee. There he saw two brothers, Simon Peter and his brother Andrew. They were throwing a net into the lake, because they were fishermen. "Come and follow me," Jesus said. "I will send you out to fish for people." At once they left their nets and followed him.

Going on from there, he saw two other brothers. They were James, son of Zebedee, and his brother John. They were in a boat with their father Zebedee. As they were preparing their nets, Jesus called out to them. Right away they left the boat and their father and followed Jesus.

Jesus went all over Galilee. There he taught in the synagogues. He preached the good news of God's kingdom. He healed every illness and sickness the people had. Large crowds followed him.

∾᠑᠑᠑᠊

Jesus saw the crowds. So he went up on a mountainside and sat down. His disciples came to him. Then he began to teach them. He said,

"Blessed are those who are spiritually needy.
The kingdom of heaven belongs to them.
Blessed are those who are sad.
They will be comforted.
Blessed are those who are humble.
They will be given the earth.
Blessed are those who are hungry and thirsty for what is right.
They will be filled.
Blessed are those who show mercy.
They will be shown mercy.
Blessed are those whose hearts are pure.
They will see God.
Blessed are those who make peace.
They will be called children of God.
Blessed are those who suffer for doing what is right.
The kingdom of heaven belongs to them.

"Blessed are you when people make fun of you and hurt you because of me. You are also blessed when they tell all kinds of evil lies about you because of me. Be joyful and glad. Your reward in heaven is great. In the same way, people hurt the prophets who lived long ago.

"You are the light of the world. A town built on a hill can't be hidden. Also, people do not light a lamp and put it under a bowl. Instead, they put it on its stand. Then it gives light to everyone in the house. In the same way, let your light shine so others can see it. Then they will see the good things you do. And they will bring glory to your Father who is in heaven.

"Do not think I have come to get rid of what is written in the Law or in the Prophets. I have not come to do this. Instead, I have come to fulfill what is written.

Do not fight against an evil person. Suppose someone slaps you on your right cheek. Turn your other cheek to them also. Suppose someone takes you to court to get your shirt. Let them have your coat also. Suppose someone forces you to go one mile. Go two miles with them.

When you pray, do not keep talking on and on. That is what ungodly people do. Your Father knows what you need even before you ask him.

"This is how you should pray.

" 'Our Father in heaven,
may your name be honored.
May your kingdom come.
May what you want to happen be done
    on earth as it is done in heaven.
Give us today our daily bread.
And forgive us our sins,
    just as we also have forgiven those who sin against us.
Keep us from sinning when we are tempted.
    Save us from the evil one.'

Forgive other people when they sin against you. If you do, your Father who is in heaven will also forgive you.

"I tell you, do not worry. Don't say, 'What will we eat?' Or, 'What will we drink?' Or, 'What will we wear?' People who are ungodly run after all those things. Your Father who is in heaven knows that you need them. But put God's kingdom first. Do what he wants you to do. Then all those things will also be given to you.

"So then, everyone who hears my words and puts them into practice is like a wise man. He builds his house on the rock. The rain comes down. The water rises. The winds blow and beat against that house. But it does not fall. It is built on the rock. But everyone who hears my words and does not put them into practice is like a foolish man. He builds his house on sand. The rain comes down. The water rises. The winds blow and beat against that house. And it falls with a loud crash."

Jesus finished saying all these things. The crowds were amazed at his teaching. That's because he taught like one who had authority. He did not speak like their teachers of the law.

remember what you read

1. What is something you noticed for the first time?

_____

_____

_____

_____

2. What questions did you have?

_____

_____

_____

_____

3. Was there anything that bothered you?

_____

_____

_____

_____

4. What did you learn about loving God?

_____

_____

_____

_____

5. What did you learn about loving others?

_____

_____

_____

_____

introduction to Matthew, part 2

In the first reading of Matthew's story, Jesus wowed the people with his teaching. He taught with authority, like someone who actually knew what they were talking about. In other words, Jesus stood head and shoulders above the religious leaders of his day, which didn't sit too well with the religious leaders.

In today's reading, Jesus continues to show his power. But how long will the authorities just sit there and take it?

Things are getting dangerous for Jesus and his friends. John, the one who baptized Jesus, is thrown in jail by Herod Antipas, son of the king who tried to kill Jesus as a baby.

Jesus came down from the mountainside. Large crowds followed him. A man who had a skin disease came and got down on his knees in front of Jesus. He said, "Lord, if you are willing to make me 'clean,' you can do it."

Jesus reached out his hand and touched the man. "I am willing to do it," he said. "Be 'clean'!" Right away the man was healed of his skin disease. Then Jesus said to him, "Don't tell anyone. Go and show yourself to the priest, and offer the gift Moses commanded. It will be a witness to everyone."

When Jesus entered Capernaum, a Roman commander came to him. He asked Jesus for help. "Lord," he said, "my servant lies at home and can't move. He is suffering terribly."

Jesus said, "Shall I come and heal him?"

The commander replied, "Lord, I am not good enough to have you come into my house. But just say the word, and my servant will be healed."

When Jesus heard this, he was amazed. He said to those following him, "What I'm about to tell you is true. In Israel I have not found anyone whose faith is so strong."

Then Jesus said to the Roman commander, "Go! It will be done just as you believed it would." And his servant was healed at that moment.

⚬⚬⚬

Jesus got into a boat. His disciples followed him. Suddenly a terrible storm came up on the lake. The waves crashed over the boat. But Jesus was sleeping. The disciples went and woke him up. They said, "Lord! Save us! We're going to drown!"

He replied, "Your faith is so small! Why are you so afraid?" Then Jesus got up and ordered the winds and the waves to stop. It became completely calm.

The disciples were amazed. They asked, "What kind of man is this? Even the winds and the waves obey him!"

⚬⚬⚬

He went over to the other side of the lake and came to his own town. Some men brought to him a man who could not walk. He was lying on a mat. Jesus saw that they had faith. So he said to the man, "Don't lose hope, son. Your sins are forgiven."

The man got up and went home. When the crowd saw this, they were filled with wonder. They praised God for giving that kind of authority to a human being.

As Jesus went on from there, two blind men followed him. They called out, "Have mercy on us, Son of David!"

When Jesus went indoors, the blind men came to him. He asked them, "Do you believe that I can do this?"

"Yes, Lord," they replied.

Then he touched their eyes. He said, "It will happen to you just as you believed." They could now see again. Jesus strongly warned them, "Be sure that no one knows about this." But they went out and spread the news. They talked about him all over that area.

Jesus went through all the towns and villages. He taught in their synagogues. He preached the good news of the kingdom. And he healed every illness and sickness. When he saw the crowds, he felt deep concern for them. They were treated badly and were helpless, like sheep without a shepherd. Then Jesus said to his disciples, "The harvest is huge. But there are only a few workers. So ask the Lord of the harvest to send workers out into his harvest field."

⟡

Jesus called for his 12 disciples to come to him. He gave them authority to drive out evil spirits and to heal every illness and sickness.

Here are the names of the 12 apostles.

First there were Simon Peter and his brother Andrew.
Then came James, son of Zebedee, and his brother John.
Next were Philip and Bartholomew,
and also Thomas and Matthew the tax collector.
Two more were James, son of Alphaeus, and Thaddaeus.
The last were Simon the Zealot and Judas Iscariot. Judas was the one who was later going to hand Jesus over to his enemies.

Jesus sent these 12 out with the following orders. "Do not go among the Gentiles," he said. "Do not enter any town of the Samaritans. Instead, go to the people of Israel. They are like sheep that have become lost. As you go, preach this message, 'The kingdom of heaven has come near.' Heal those who are sick. Bring those who are dead back to life. Make those who have skin diseases 'clean' again. Drive out demons. You have received freely, so give freely."

⟡

Jesus finished teaching his 12 disciples. Then he went on to teach and preach in the towns of Galilee.

"Come to me, all you who are tired and are carrying heavy loads. I will give you rest. Become my servants and learn from me. I am gentle and free of pride. You will find rest for your souls. Serving me is easy, and my load is light."

༄༅

One Sabbath day Jesus walked through the grainfields. His disciples were hungry. So they began to break off some heads of grain and eat them. The Pharisees saw this. They said to Jesus, "Look! It is against the Law to do this on the Sabbath day. But your disciples are doing it anyway!"

Jesus answered, "Scripture says, 'I want mercy and not sacrifice.' You don't know what those words mean. If you did, you would not bring charges against those who are not guilty. The Son of Man is Lord of the Sabbath day."

Going on from that place, Jesus went into their synagogue. A man with a weak and twisted hand was there. The Pharisees were trying to accuse Jesus of a crime. So they asked him, "Does the Law allow us to heal on the Sabbath day?"

He said to them, "What if one of your sheep falls into a pit on the Sabbath day? Won't you take hold of it and lift it out? A person is worth more than sheep! So the Law allows us to do good on the Sabbath day."

Then Jesus said to the man, "Stretch out your hand." So he stretched it out. It had been made as good as new. It was just as good as the other hand. But the Pharisees went out and planned how to kill Jesus.

Jesus knew all about the Pharisees' plans. So he left that place. A large crowd followed him, and he healed all who were sick. But he warned them not to tell other people about him.

༄༅

A man controlled by demons was brought to Jesus. The man was blind and could not speak. Jesus healed him. Then the man could speak and see. All the people were amazed. They said, "Could this be the Son of David?"

The Pharisees heard this. So they said, "This fellow drives out demons by the power of Beelzebul, the prince of demons."

Jesus knew what they were thinking. So he said to them, "Every kingdom that fights against itself will be destroyed. Every city or family that is divided against itself will not stand. If Satan drives out Satan, he fights against himself. Then how can his kingdom stand?

"Anyone who is not with me is against me. Anyone who does not gather sheep with me scatters them.

⌒⟲⟲⌒

That same day Jesus left the house and sat by the Sea of Galilee. Large crowds gathered around him. Then he told them many things using stories.

The disciples came to him. They asked, "Why do you use stories when you speak to the people?"

He replied, "Because you have been given the knowledge of the secrets of the kingdom of heaven. It has not been given to outsiders.

But blessed are your eyes because they see. And blessed are your ears because they hear. What I'm about to tell you is true. Many prophets and godly people wanted to see what you see. But they didn't see it. They wanted to hear what you hear. But they didn't hear it.

"The kingdom of heaven is like treasure that was hidden in a field. When a man found it, he hid it again. He was very happy. So he went and sold everything he had. And he bought that field.

"Again, the kingdom of heaven is like a trader who was looking for fine pearls. He found one that was very valuable. So he went away and sold everything he had. And he bought that pearl.

"Again, the kingdom of heaven is like a net. It was let down into the lake. It caught all kinds of fish. When it was full, the fishermen pulled it up on the shore. Then they sat down and gathered the good fish into baskets. But they threw the bad fish away. This is how it will be on judgment day. The angels will come. They will separate the people who did what is wrong from those who did what is right. They will throw the evil people into the blazing furnace. There the evil ones will weep and grind their teeth.

"Do you understand all these things?" Jesus asked.

"Yes," they replied.

He said to them, "Every teacher of the law who has become a disciple in the kingdom of heaven is like the owner of a house. He brings new treasures out of his storeroom as well as old ones."

On Herod's birthday the daughter of Herodias danced for Herod and his guests. She pleased Herod very much. So he promised to give her anything she asked for. Her mother told her what to say. So the girl said to Herod, "Give me the head of John the Baptist on a big plate." The king was very upset. But he thought of his promise and his dinner guests. So he told one of his men to give her what she asked for. Herod had John's head cut off in the prison. His head was brought in on a big plate and given to the girl. She then carried it to her mother. John's disciples came and took his body and buried it. Then they went and told Jesus.

remember what you read

1. What is something you noticed for the first time?

_____

_____

_____

_____

2. What questions did you have?

_____

_____

_____

_____

3. Was there anything that bothered you?

_____

_____

_____

_____

4. What did you learn about loving God?

_____

_____

_____

_____

5. What did you learn about loving others?

_____

_____

_____

_____

MATTHEW, PART 3

introduction to Matthew, part 3

Even though things are getting dangerous, Jesus isn't about to give up on his mission. He's busy making a new kingdom where everyone is welcome: the hungry, the sick, outsiders, children. He calls it the "kingdom of heaven." As you read, see if you can count how many times Jesus uses this phrase.

Jesus heard what had happened to John. He wanted to be alone. So he went in a boat to a quiet place. The crowds heard about this. They followed him on foot from the towns. When Jesus came ashore, he saw a large crowd. He felt deep concern for them. He healed their sick people.

When it was almost evening, the disciples came to him. "There is nothing here," they said. "It's already getting late. Send the crowds away. They can go and buy some food in the villages."

Jesus replied, "They don't need to go away. You give them something to eat."

"We have only five loaves of bread and two fish," they answered.

"Bring them here to me," he said. Then Jesus directed the people to sit down on the grass. He took the five loaves and the two fish. He looked up to heaven and gave thanks. He broke the loaves into pieces. Then he gave them to the disciples. And the disciples gave them to the people. All of them ate and were satisfied. The disciples picked up 12 baskets of leftover pieces. The number of men who ate was about 5,000. Women and children also ate.

Right away Jesus made the disciples get into the boat. He had them go on ahead of him to the other side of the Sea of Galilee. Then he sent the crowd away. After he had sent them away, he went up on a mountainside by himself to pray. Later that night, he was there alone. The boat was already a long way from land. It was being pounded by the waves because the wind was blowing against it.

Shortly before dawn, Jesus went out to the disciples. He walked on the lake. They saw him walking on the lake and were terrified. "It's a ghost!" they said. And they cried out in fear.

Right away Jesus called out to them, "Be brave! It is I. Don't be afraid."

"Lord, is it you?" Peter asked. "If it is, tell me to come to you on the water."

"Come," Jesus said.

So Peter got out of the boat. He walked on the water toward Jesus. But when Peter saw the wind, he was afraid. He began to sink. He cried out, "Lord! Save me!"

Right away Jesus reached out his hand and caught him. "Your faith is so small!" he said. "Why did you doubt me?"

When they climbed into the boat, the wind died down. Then those in the boat worshiped Jesus. They said, "You really are the Son of God!"

They crossed over the lake and landed at Gennesaret.

Jesus left Galilee and went to the area of Tyre and Sidon. A woman from Canaan lived near Tyre and Sidon. She came to him and cried out, "Lord! Son of David! Have mercy on me! A demon controls my daughter. She is suffering terribly."

Jesus did not say a word. So his disciples came to him. They begged him, "Send her away. She keeps crying out after us."

Jesus answered, "I was sent only to the people of Israel."

Then the woman fell to her knees in front of him. "Lord! Help me!" she said.

He replied, "It is not right to take the children's bread and throw it to the dogs."

"Yes it is, Lord," she said. "Even the dogs eat the crumbs that fall from their owner's table."

Then Jesus said to her, "Woman, you have great faith! You will be given what you are asking for." And her daughter was healed at that moment.

Jesus left there. He walked along the Sea of Galilee. Then he went up on a mountainside and sat down. Large crowds came to him. They brought blind people and those who could not walk. They also brought disabled people, those who could not speak, and many others. They laid them at his feet, and he healed them. The people were amazed. Those who could not speak were speaking. The disabled were made well. Those not able to walk were walking. Those who were blind could see. So the people praised the God of Israel.

~~~

Jesus went to the area of Caesarea Philippi. There he asked his disciples, "Who do people say the Son of Man is?"

They replied, "Some say John the Baptist. Others say Elijah. Still others say Jeremiah, or one of the prophets."

"But what about you?" he asked. "Who do you say I am?"

Simon Peter answered, "You are the Messiah. You are the Son of the living God."

Jesus replied, "Blessed are you, Simon, son of Jonah! No mere human showed this to you. My Father in heaven showed it to you. Here is what I tell you. You are Peter. On this rock I will build my church. The gates of hell will not be strong enough to destroy it. I will give you the keys to the kingdom of heaven. What you lock on earth will be locked in heaven. What you unlock on earth will be unlocked in heaven." Then Jesus ordered his disciples not to tell anyone that he was the Messiah.

~~~

After six days Jesus took Peter, James, and John the brother of James with him. He led them up a high mountain. They were all alone. There in front of them his appearance was changed. His face shone like the sun. His clothes became as white as the light. Just then Moses and Elijah appeared in front of them. Moses and Elijah were talking with Jesus.

Peter said to Jesus, "Lord, it is good for us to be here. If you wish, I will put up three shelters. One will be for you, one for Moses, and one for Elijah."

While Peter was still speaking, a bright cloud covered them. A voice from the cloud said, "This is my Son, and I love him. I am very pleased with him. Listen to him!"

When the disciples heard this, they were terrified. They fell with their faces to the ground. But Jesus came and touched them. "Get up," he said. "Don't be afraid." When they looked up, they saw no one except Jesus.

They came down the mountain. On the way down, Jesus told them what to do. "Don't tell anyone what you have seen," he said. "Wait until the Son of Man has been raised from the dead."

∽༄༄༄∽

When they came near the crowd, a man approached Jesus. He got on his knees in front of him. "Lord," he said, "have mercy on my son. He shakes wildly and suffers a great deal. He often falls into the fire or into the water. I brought him to your disciples. But they couldn't heal him."

"You unbelieving and evil people!" Jesus replied. "How long do I have to stay with you? How long do I have to put up with you? Bring the boy here to me." Jesus ordered the demon to leave the boy, and it came out of him. He was healed at that moment.

Then the disciples came to Jesus in private. They asked, "Why couldn't we drive out the demon?"

He replied, "Because your faith is much too small. What I'm about to tell you is true. If you have faith as small as a mustard seed, it is enough. You can say to this mountain, 'Move from here to there.' And it will move. Nothing will be impossible for you."

At that time the disciples came to Jesus. They asked him, "Then who is the most important person in the kingdom of heaven?" Jesus called a little child over to him. He had the child stand among them. Jesus said, "What I'm about to tell you is true. You need to change and become like little children. If you don't, you will never enter the kingdom of heaven. Anyone who takes the humble position of this child is the most important in the kingdom of heaven. Anyone who welcomes a little child like this one in my name welcomes me.

"See that you don't look down on one of these little ones. Here is what I tell you. Their angels in heaven are always with my Father who is in heaven.

"What do you think? Suppose a man owns 100 sheep and one of them wanders away. Won't he leave the 99 sheep on the hills? Won't he go and look for the one that wandered off? What I'm about to tell you is true. If he finds that sheep, he is happier about the one than about the 99 that didn't wander off. It is the same with your Father in heaven. He does not want any of these little ones to die.

Peter came to Jesus. He asked, "Lord, how many times should I forgive my brother or sister who sins against me? Up to seven times?"

Jesus answered, "I tell you, not seven times, but 77 times.

"The kingdom of heaven is like a king who wanted to collect all the money his servants owed him. As the king began to do it, a man who owed him 10,000 bags of gold was brought to him. The man was not able to pay. So his master gave an order. The man, his wife, his children, and all he owned had to be sold to pay back what he owed.

"Then the servant fell on his knees in front of him. 'Give me time,' he begged. 'I'll pay everything back.' His master felt sorry for him. He forgave him what he owed and let him go.

"But then that servant went out and found one of the other servants who owed him 100 silver coins. He grabbed him and began to choke him. 'Pay back what you owe me!' he said.

"The other servant fell on his knees. 'Give me time,' he begged him. 'I'll pay it back.'

"But the first servant refused. Instead, he went and had the man thrown into prison. The man would be held there until he could pay back what he owed. The other servants saw what had happened and were very angry. They went and told their master everything that had happened.

"Then the master called the first servant in. 'You evil servant,' he said. 'I forgave all that you owed me because you begged me to. Shouldn't you have had mercy on the other servant just as I had mercy on you?' In anger his master handed him over to the jailers. He would be punished until he paid back everything he owed.

"This is how my Father in heaven will treat each of you unless you forgive your brother or sister from your heart."

༄

When Jesus finished saying these things, he left Galilee. He went into the area of Judea on the other side of the Jordan River. Large crowds followed him. He healed them there.

Some people brought little children to Jesus. They wanted him to place his hands on the children and pray for them. But the disciples told them not to do it.

Jesus said, "Let the little children come to me. Don't keep them away. The kingdom of heaven belongs to people like them." Jesus placed his hands on them to bless them. Then he went on from there.

remember what you read

1. What is something you noticed for the first time?

_____

_____

_____

_____

2. What questions did you have?

_____

_____

_____

_____

3. Was there anything that bothered you?

_____

_____

_____

_____

4. What did you learn about loving God?

_____

_____

_____

_____

5. What did you learn about loving others?

_____

_____

_____

_____

introduction to Matthew, part 4

Things are heating up between Jesus and the religious leaders. Today, we'll read part four of Matthew's story. In it, Jesus makes his way to Jerusalem. But the religious leaders, who feel threatened by his popularity, are setting a trap. Will they catch Jesus off-guard? Or does Jesus know exactly what he's getting into? Read to find out.

ↄ҈ↄ

Just then, a man came up to Jesus. He asked, "Teacher, what good thing must I do to receive eternal life?"

"Why do you ask me about what is good?" Jesus replied. "There is only one who is good. If you want to enter the kingdom, obey the commandments."

"Which ones?" the man asked.

Jesus said, " 'Do not murder. Do not commit adultery. Do not steal. Do not be a false witness. Honor your father and mother.' And 'love your neighbor as you love yourself.' "

"I have obeyed all those commandments," the young man said. "What else do I need to do?"

Jesus answered, "If you want to be perfect, go and sell everything you have. Give the money to those who are poor. You will have treasure in heaven. Then come and follow me."

When the young man heard this, he went away sad. He was very rich.

Then Jesus said to his disciples, "What I'm about to tell you is true. It is hard for someone who is rich to enter the kingdom of heaven."

When the disciples heard this, they were really amazed. They asked, "Then who can be saved?"

Jesus looked at them and said, "With people, this is impossible. But with God, all things are possible."

∽ʊʊ∾

Jesus was going up to Jerusalem. On the way, he took his 12 disciples to one side to talk to them. "We are going up to Jerusalem," he said. "The Son of Man will be handed over to the chief priests and the teachers of the law. They will sentence him to death. Then they will hand him over to the Gentiles. The people will make fun of him and whip him. They will nail him to a cross. On the third day, he will rise from the dead!"

When Jesus entered Jerusalem, the whole city was stirred up. The people asked, "Who is this?"

The crowds answered, "This is Jesus. He is the prophet from Nazareth in Galilee."

Jesus entered the temple courtyard. He began to drive out all those who were buying and selling there. He turned over the tables of the people who were exchanging money. He also turned over the benches of those who were selling doves. He said to them, "It is written that the Lord said, 'My house will be called a house where people can pray.' But you are making it 'a den for robbers.'"

Blind people and those who were disabled came to Jesus at the temple. There he healed them. The chief priests and the teachers of the law saw the wonderful things he did. But when they saw all this, they became angry.

They made plans to trap Jesus with his own words. "Teacher," they said, "we know that you are a man of honor. Tell us then, what do you think? Is it right to pay the royal tax to Caesar or not?"

But Jesus knew their evil plans. He said, "You pretenders! Why are you trying to trap me? Show me the coin people use for paying the tax." They brought him a silver coin. He asked them, "Whose picture is this? And whose words?"

"Caesar's," they replied.

Then he said to them, "So give back to Caesar what belongs to Caesar. And give back to God what belongs to God."

When they heard this, they were amazed.

One of them was an authority on the law. So he tested Jesus with a question. "Teacher," he asked, "which is the most important commandment in the Law?"

Jesus replied, " 'Love the Lord your God with all your heart and with all your soul. Love him with all your mind.' This is the first and most important commandment. And the second is like it. 'Love your neighbor as you love yourself.' Everything that is written in the Law and the Prophets is based on these two commandments."

Jesus spoke to the crowds and to his disciples. "The teachers of the law and the Pharisees sit in Moses' seat," he said. "So you must be careful to do everything they say. But don't do what they do. They don't practice what they preach. They tie up heavy loads that are hard to carry. Then they put them on other people's shoulders. But they themselves aren't willing to lift a finger to move them.

"Everything they do is done for others to see. They love to sit down in the place of honor at dinners. They also love to have the most important seats in the synagogues.

"How terrible it will be for you, teachers of the law and Pharisees! You pretenders! You shut the door of the kingdom of heaven in people's faces. You yourselves do not enter. And you will not let those enter who are trying to.

"How terrible for you, teachers of the law and Pharisees! You pretenders! You give God a tenth of your spices, like mint, dill and cumin. But you have not practiced the more important things of the law, which are fairness, mercy and faithfulness. You should have practiced the last things without failing to do the first.

"How terrible for you, teachers of the law and Pharisees! You pretenders! You clean the outside of a cup and dish. But on the inside you are full of greed. You only want to satisfy yourselves.

"You nest of poisonous snakes! How will you escape from being sentenced to hell? So I am sending you prophets, wise people, and teachers. You will kill some of them. You will nail some to a cross. Others you will whip in your synagogues. You will chase them from town to town.

"Jerusalem! Jerusalem! You kill the prophets and throw stones in order to kill those who are sent to you. Many times I have wanted to gather your people together. I have wanted to be like a hen who gathers her chicks under her wings. And you would not let me! Look, your house is left empty. I tell you, you will not see me again until you say, 'Blessed is the one who comes in the name of the Lord.'"

⟆⟆⟆

Jesus left the temple. The disciples came to him in private. "Tell us," they said. "When will this happen? And what will be the sign of your coming? What will be the sign of the end?"

Jesus answered, "Keep watch! Be careful that no one fools you. Many will come in my name. They will claim, 'I am the Messiah!' They will fool many people. You will hear about wars. You will also hear people talking about future wars. Don't be alarmed. Those things must happen. But the end still isn't here. Nation will fight against nation. Kingdom will fight against kingdom. People will go hungry. There will be earthquakes in many places. All these are the beginning of birth pains.

"Then people will hand you over to be treated badly and killed. All nations will hate you because of me. Because evil will grow, most people's love will grow cold. But the one who remains strong in the faith will be saved. This good news of the kingdom will be preached in the whole world. It will be a witness to all nations. Then the end will come.

"But no one knows about that day or hour. Not even the angels in heaven know. The Son does not know. Only the Father knows.

"So keep watch. You do not know on what day your Lord will come.

"The Son of Man will come in all his glory. All the nations will be gathered in front of him. He will separate the people into two groups. He will be like a shepherd who separates the sheep from the goats. He will put the sheep to his right and the goats to his left.

"Then the King will speak to those on his right. He will say, 'My Father has blessed you. Come and take what is yours. It is the kingdom prepared for you since the world was created. I was hungry.

And you gave me something to eat. I was thirsty. And you gave me something to drink. I was a stranger. And you invited me in. I needed clothes. And you gave them to me. I was sick. And you took care of me. I was in prison. And you came to visit me.'

"Then the people who have done what is right will answer him. 'Lord,' they will ask, 'when did we see you hungry and feed you? When did we see you thirsty and give you something to drink? When did we see you as a stranger and invite you in? When did we see you needing clothes and give them to you? When did we see you sick or in prison and go to visit you?'

"The King will reply, 'What I'm about to tell you is true. Anything you did for one of the least important of these brothers and sisters of mine, you did for me.'

"Then he will say to those on his left, 'You are cursed! Go away from me into the fire that burns forever. It has been prepared for the devil and his angels. I was hungry. But you gave me nothing to eat. I was thirsty. But you gave me nothing to drink. I was a stranger. But you did not invite me in. I needed clothes. But you did not give me any. I was sick and in prison. But you did not take care of me.'

"They also will answer, 'Lord, when did we see you hungry or thirsty and not help you? When did we see you as a stranger or needing clothes or sick or in prison and not help you?'

"He will reply, 'What I'm about to tell you is true. Anything you didn't do for one of the least important of these, you didn't do for me.'

"Then they will go away to be punished forever. But those who have done what is right will receive eternal life."

◌ᢙᢍᢙ◌

Jesus finished saying all these things. Then he said to his disciples, "As you know, the Passover Feast is two days away. The Son of Man will be handed over to be nailed to a cross."

Then the chief priests met with the elders of the people. They met in the palace of Caiaphas, the high priest. They made plans to arrest Jesus secretly. They wanted to kill him.

One of the 12 disciples went to the chief priests. His name was Judas Iscariot. He asked, "What will you give me if I hand Jesus over to you?" So they counted out 30 silver coins for him.

༚༚༚

When evening came, Jesus was at the table with his 12 disciples. While they were eating, he said, "What I'm about to tell you is true. One of you will hand me over to my enemies."

Judas was the one who was going to hand him over. He said, "Surely you don't mean me, Teacher, do you?"

Jesus answered, "You have said so."

While they were eating, Jesus took bread. He gave thanks and broke it. He handed it to his disciples and said, "Take this and eat it. This is my body."

Then he took a cup. He gave thanks and handed it to them. He said, "All of you drink from it. This is my blood of the covenant. It is poured out to forgive the sins of many people.

Then they sang a hymn and went out to the Mount of Olives.

remember what you read

1. What is something you noticed for the first time?

_____

_____

_____

_____

2. What questions did you have?

_____

_____

_____

_____

3. Was there anything that bothered you?

_____

_____

_____

_____

4. What did you learn about loving God?

_____

_____

_____

_____

5. What did you learn about loving others?

_____

_____

_____

_____

MATTHEW, PART 5

introduction to Matthew, part 5

Jesus is on his way to Jerusalem. He's going for one reason: to lay down his life. The religious leaders who want Jesus killed think they're calling the shots. But as you read, see if you can tell who's really in control.

ᘜᘜᘜ

Jesus told them, "This very night you will all turn away because of me. It is written that the Lord said,

" 'I will strike the shepherd down.
   Then the sheep of the flock will be scattered.'

But after I rise from the dead, I will go ahead of you into Galilee."

Peter replied, "All the others may turn away because of you. But I never will."

"What I'm about to tell you is true," Jesus answered. "It will happen tonight. Before the rooster crows, you will say three times that you don't know me."

Then Jesus went with his disciples to a place called Gethsemane. He said to them, "Sit here while I go over there and pray." He took Peter and the two sons of Zebedee along with him. He began to be sad and troubled. Then he said to them, "My soul is very sad. I feel close to death. Stay here. Keep watch with me."

He went a little farther. Then he fell with his face to the ground. He prayed, "My Father, if it is possible, take this cup of suffering away from me. But let what you want be done, not what I want."

Then he returned to his disciples and found them sleeping.

"Couldn't you men keep watch with me for one hour?" he asked Peter. "Watch and pray."

Jesus went away a second time. He prayed.

Then he came back. Again he found them sleeping. So he left them and went away once more. For the third time he prayed the same thing.

Then he returned to the disciples. He said to them, "Are you still sleeping and resting? Look! The hour has come. The Son of Man is about to be handed over to sinners."

While Jesus was still speaking, Judas arrived. He was one of the 12 disciples. A large crowd was with him. They were carrying swords and clubs. The chief priests and the elders of the people had sent them. Judas, who was going to hand Jesus over, had arranged a signal with them. "The one I kiss is the man," he said. "Arrest him." So Judas went to Jesus at once. He said, "Greetings, Rabbi!" And he kissed him.

Jesus replied, "Friend, do what you came to do."

Then the men stepped forward. They grabbed Jesus and arrested him. At that moment, one of Jesus' companions reached for his sword. He pulled it out and struck the slave of the high priest with it. He cut off the slave's ear.

"Put your sword back in its place," Jesus said to him. "All who use the sword will die by the sword. Do you think I can't ask my Father for help? He would send an army of more than 70,000 angels right away. But then how would the Scriptures come true? They say it must happen in this way."

Then all the disciples left him and ran away.

⚬ᴓᴓ⌐

Those who had arrested Jesus took him to Caiaphas, the high priest. The teachers of the law and the elders had come together there. The high priest said to him, "I am commanding you in the name of the living God. May he judge you if you don't tell the truth. Tell us if you are the Messiah, the Son of God."

"You have said so," Jesus replied. "But here is what I say to all of you. From now on, you will see the Son of Man sitting at the right hand of the Mighty One. You will see the Son of Man coming on the clouds of heaven."

Then the high priest tore his clothes. He said, "Why do we need any more witnesses? You have heard him say this evil thing. What do you think?"

"He must die!" they answered.

Then they spit in his face. They hit him with their fists. Others slapped him.

❧

Peter was sitting out in the courtyard. A female servant came to him. "You also were with Jesus of Galilee," she said.

But in front of all of them, Peter said he was not.

Then he went out to the gate leading into the courtyard. There another servant saw him. She said to the people, "This fellow was with Jesus of Nazareth."

Again he said he was not.

After a little while, those standing there went up to Peter. "You must be one of them," they said.

Then Peter began to curse and said to them, "I don't know the man!"

Right away a rooster crowed. Then Peter remembered what Jesus had said. Peter went outside. He broke down and cried.

❧

It was early in the morning. All the chief priests and the elders of the people planned how to put Jesus to death. So they tied him up and led him away. Then they handed him over to Pilate, who was the governor.

Judas, who had handed him over, saw that Jesus had been sentenced to die. He felt deep shame and sadness for what he had done. So he returned the 30 silver coins to the chief priests and the elders. "I have sinned," he said. "I handed over a man who is not guilty."

"What do we care?" they replied. "That's your problem."

So Judas threw the money into the temple and left. Then he went away and hanged himself.

＊＊＊

Jesus was standing in front of the governor. The governor asked him, "Are you the king of the Jews?"

"Yes. You have said so," Jesus replied.

But when the chief priests and the elders brought charges against him, he did not answer. Then Pilate asked him, "Don't you hear the charges they are bringing against you?" But Jesus made no reply, not even to a single charge. The governor was really amazed.

It was the governor's practice at the Passover Feast to let one prisoner go free. The people could choose the one they wanted. At that time they had a well-known prisoner named Jesus Barabbas. So when the crowd gathered, Pilate asked them, "Which one do you want me to set free? Jesus Barabbas? Or Jesus who is called the Messiah?"

But the chief priests and the elders talked the crowd into asking for Barabbas and having Jesus put to death.

"Barabbas," they answered.

"Then what should I do with Jesus who is called the Messiah?" Pilate asked.

They all answered, "Crucify him!"

"Why? What wrong has he done?" asked Pilate.

But they shouted even louder, "Crucify him!"

Pilate let Barabbas go free. But he had Jesus whipped. Then he handed him over to be nailed to a cross.

＊＊＊

The governor's soldiers took Jesus into the palace. They took off his clothes and put a purple robe on him. Then they twisted thorns together to make a crown. They placed it on his head. They put a stick in his right hand. Then they fell on their knees in front of him and made fun of him. "We honor you, king of the Jews!" they said. They spit on him. They hit him on the head with the stick again and again. After they had made fun of him, they took off the robe. They put his own clothes back on him. Then they led him away to nail him to a cross.

They came to a place called Golgotha. When they had nailed him to the cross, they divided up his clothes by casting lots. Above his head they placed the written charge against him. It read,

THIS IS JESUS, THE KING OF THE JEWS.

From noon until three o'clock, the whole land was covered with darkness. About three o'clock, Jesus cried out in a loud voice. "My God, my God, why have you deserted me?"

After Jesus cried out again in a loud voice, he died.

At that moment the temple curtain was torn in two from top to bottom. The earth shook. The rocks split. Tombs broke open. The bodies of many holy people who had died were raised to life. The Roman commander and those guarding Jesus saw the earthquake and all that had happened. They were terrified. They exclaimed, "He was surely the Son of God!"

As evening approached, a rich man came from the town of Arimathea. His name was Joseph. He had become a follower of Jesus. He went to Pilate and asked for Jesus' body. Pilate ordered that it be given to him. Joseph took the body and wrapped it in a clean linen cloth. He placed it in his own new tomb that he had cut out of the rock. He rolled a big stone in front of the entrance to the tomb. Then he went away.

The chief priests and the Pharisees went to Pilate. "Sir," they said, "we remember something that liar said while he was still alive. He claimed, 'After three days I will rise again.' So give the order to make the tomb secure until the third day. If you don't, his disciples might come and steal the body. Then they will tell the people that Jesus has been raised from the dead. This last lie will be worse than the first."

"Take some guards with you," Pilate answered. "Go. Make the tomb as secure as you can." So they went and made the tomb secure. They put a royal seal on the stone and placed some guards on duty.

ॐ

The Sabbath day was now over. It was dawn on the first day of the week. Mary Magdalene and the other Mary went to look at the tomb.

There was a powerful earthquake. An angel of the Lord came down from heaven. The angel went to the tomb. He rolled back the stone and sat on it. His body shone like lightning. The guards were so afraid of him that they shook and became like dead men.

The angel said to the women, "Don't be afraid. I know that you are looking for Jesus, who was crucified. He is not here! He has risen, just as he said he would! Come and see the place where he was lying. Go quickly! Tell his disciples, 'He has risen from the dead.' "

So the women hurried away from the tomb. They were afraid, but they were filled with joy. They ran to tell the disciples. Suddenly Jesus met them. "Greetings!" he said. They came to him, took hold of his feet and worshiped him. Then Jesus said to them, "Don't be afraid. Go and tell my brothers to go to Galilee. There they will see me."

ॐ

Then the 11 disciples went to Galilee. They went to the mountain where Jesus had told them to go. When they saw him, they worshiped him. But some still had their doubts. Then Jesus came to them. He said, "All authority in heaven and on earth has been given to me. So you must go and make disciples of all nations. Baptize them in the name of the Father and of the Son and of the Holy Spirit. Teach them to obey everything I have commanded you. And you can be sure that I am always with you, to the very end."

remember what you read

1. What is something you noticed for the first time?

_____

_____

_____

_____

2. What questions did you have?

_____

_____

_____

_____

3. Was there anything that bothered you?

_____

_____

_____

_____

4. What did you learn about loving God?

_____

_____

_____

_____

5. What did you learn about loving others?

_____

_____

_____

_____

introduction to Hebrews, part 1

After Jesus rose from the dead, lots of people started following him. Many of them were Jewish, just like Jesus. And sometimes, they had a difficult choice to make.

In the Roman Empire, some religions were allowed, but others were not. The religion of most Jewish people, known as Judaism, was legal. But what if you were a Jewish person who decided to follow Jesus? Then you could get into serious trouble.

During this time, many Jewish followers of Jesus suffered because of their faith and were tempted to hide their Christian identity. The letter you're about to read, known as the book of Hebrews, was written to encourage them to stay true to Jesus.

We don't know much more about the people who received this letter. And we don't know who wrote it, either. But according to this mystery writer, Jesus is better than anything. He's a better messenger than the angels are. He's a better leader than Moses, the famous hero who led the Israelites out of slavery. Jesus promises to give people rest and comfort that's way better than anything they've ever known.

If we want to enjoy all that Jesus has to offer, we need to stay true to him. That's the message of Hebrews. As you read, think about what makes it hard for you to follow Jesus. Ask yourself: are you willing to stay true to him, no matter what?

In the past, God spoke to our people through the prophets. He spoke at many times. He spoke in different ways. But in these last days, he has spoken to us through his Son. He is the one whom God appointed to receive all things. God also made everything through him. The Son is the shining brightness of God's glory. He is the exact likeness of God's being. He uses his powerful word to hold all things together. He provided the way for people to be made pure from sin. Then he sat down at the right hand of the King, the Majesty in heaven. So he became higher than the angels. The name he received is more excellent than theirs.

God never said to any of the angels,

"You are my Son.
Today I have become your Father."

God's first and only Son is over all things. When God brings him into the world, he says,

"Let all God's angels worship him."

Here is something else God says about the angels.

"God makes his angels to be like spirits.
He makes those who serve him to be like flashes of
lightning."

But here is what he says about the Son.

"You are God. Your throne will last for ever and ever.
Your kingdom will be ruled by justice.

God never said to an angel,

"Sit at my right hand
until I put your enemies
under your control."

All angels are spirits who serve. God sends them to serve those who will receive salvation.

So we must pay the most careful attention to what we have heard. Then we will not drift away from it. Even the message God spoke through angels had to be obeyed. Every time people broke the Law, they were punished. Every time they didn't obey, they were punished. Then how will we escape if we don't pay attention to God's great salvation? The Lord first announced this salvation. Those who heard him gave us the message about it. God showed that this message is true by signs and wonders. He showed that it's true by different kinds of miracles. God also showed that this message is true by the gifts of the Holy Spirit. God gave them out as it pleased him.

God has not put angels in charge of the world that is going to come. We are talking about that world. There is a place where someone has spoken about this. He said,

"What are human beings that you think about them?
    What is a son of man that you take care of him?
You made them a little lower than the angels.
    You placed on them a crown of glory and honor.
    You have put everything under their control."

So God has put everything under his Son. Everything is under his control. We do not now see everything under his control. But we do see Jesus already given a crown of glory and honor. He was made lower than the angels for a little while. He suffered death. By the grace of God, he tasted death for everyone. That is why he was given his crown.

God has made everything. He is now bringing his many sons and daughters to share in his glory. It is only right that Jesus is the one to lead them into their salvation. That's because God made him perfect by his sufferings. And Jesus, who makes people holy, and the people he makes holy belong to the same family. So Jesus is not ashamed to call them his brothers and sisters.

So Jesus became human like them in order to die for them. By doing this, he could break the power of the devil. The devil is the one who rules over the kingdom of death. Jesus could set people free who were afraid of death. All their lives they were held as slaves by that fear. It is certainly Abraham's children that he helps. He doesn't help angels. So he had to be made like people, fully human in every way. Then he could serve God as a kind and faithful high priest. And then he could pay for the sins of the people by dying for them. He himself suffered when he was tempted. Now he is able to help others who are being tempted.

Holy brothers and sisters, God chose you to be his people. So keep thinking about Jesus. We embrace him as our apostle and our high priest. Moses was faithful in everything he did in the house of God. In the same way, Jesus was faithful to the God who appointed him. The person who builds a house has greater honor than the house itself. In the same way, Jesus has been found worthy of greater honor than Moses. Every house is built by someone. But God is the builder of everything. "Moses was faithful as one who serves in the house of God." He was a witness to what God would say in days to come. But Christ is faithful as the Son over the house of God. And we are his house if we hold tightly to what we are certain about. We must also hold tightly to the hope we boast in.

The Holy Spirit says,

"Listen to his voice today.
　If you hear it, don't be stubborn.
You were stubborn when you opposed me.
　You did that when you were tested in the desert.
There your people of long ago tested me.
　Yet for 40 years they saw what I did.
That is why I was angry with them.
　I said, 'Their hearts are always going astray.
　They have not known my ways.'
So when I was angry, I made a promise.
　I said, 'They will never enjoy the rest I planned for them.' "

Brothers and sisters, make sure that none of you has a sinful heart. Do not let an unbelieving heart turn you away from the living God. But build one another up every day. Do it as long as there is still time. Then none of you will become stubborn. You won't be fooled by sin's tricks. We belong to Christ if we hold tightly to the faith we had at first. But we must hold it tightly until the end. It has just been said,

"Listen to his voice today.
　If you hear it, don't be stubborn.
You were stubborn when you opposed me."

Who were those who heard and refused to obey? Weren't they all the people Moses led out of Egypt? Who was God angry with for 40 years? Wasn't it with those who sinned? They died in the desert. God promised that those people would never enjoy the rest he planned for them. God gave his word when he made that promise. Didn't he make that promise to those who didn't obey? So we see that they weren't able to enter. That's because they didn't believe.

God's promise of enjoying his rest still stands. So be careful that none of you fails to receive it. The good news was announced to our people of long ago. It has also been preached to us. The message they heard didn't have any value for them. That's because they didn't share the faith of those who obeyed. Now we who have believed enjoy that rest.

But those who had the good news announced to them earlier didn't go in. That's because they didn't obey. So God again chose a certain day. He named it Today. Here is what was written in the Scripture already given.

"Listen to his voice today.
If you hear it, don't be stubborn."

So there is still a Sabbath rest for God's people. So let us make every effort to enjoy that rest. Then no one will die by disobeying as they did.

The word of God is alive and active. It is sharper than any sword that has two edges. It cuts deep enough to separate soul from spirit. It can separate bones from joints. It judges the thoughts and purposes of the heart. Nothing God created is hidden from him. His eyes see everything. He will hold us responsible for everything we do.

remember what you read

1. What is something you noticed for the first time?

_____

_____

_____

_____

2. What questions did you have?

_____

_____

_____

_____

3. Was there anything that bothered you?

_____

_____

_____

_____

4. What did you learn about loving God?

_____

_____

_____

_____

5. What did you learn about loving others?

_____

_____

_____

_____

introduction to Hebrews, part 2

Before Jesus came, God's people had specially chosen leaders called priests. Their job was to offer sacrifices to God to pay for the people's sin.

But there was a problem. People kept on sinning, so priests had to keep on sacrificing animals. We needed someone who could make us right with God once and for all.

According to the writer of Hebrews, Jesus is that person. He is our great high priest. He makes it possible for us to approach God's throne ourselves.

This letter was written to Jewish followers of Jesus who were thinking about going back to their old way of doing things. "Hang on!," the writer says. "The new is so much greater than the old. It doesn't get any better than Jesus!"

∽∾∽

We have a great high priest. He has gone up into heaven. He is Jesus the Son of God. So let us hold firmly to what we say we believe. We have a high priest who can feel it when we are weak and hurting. We have a high priest who has been tempted in every way, just as we are. But he did not sin. So let us boldly approach God's throne of grace. Then we will receive mercy. We will find grace to help us when we need it.

Every high priest is chosen from among the people. He is appointed to act for the people. He acts for them in whatever has to do with God. He offers gifts and sacrifices for their sins. And no one can take this honor for himself. Instead, he receives it when he is appointed by God.

It was the same for Christ. He did not take for himself the glory of becoming a high priest. God appointed him to be the high priest.

He is the go-between for the new covenant. This covenant is better than the old one. The new covenant is based on better promises.

Suppose nothing had been wrong with that first covenant. Then no one would have looked for another covenant. But God found fault with the people. He said,

"The days are coming, announces the Lord.
I will make a new covenant
with the people of Israel.
I will also make it with the people of Judah.
It will not be like the covenant
I made with their people of long ago.
I will put my laws in their minds.
I will write them on their hearts.
I will be their God.
And they will be my people.
Everyone will know me.
From the least important to the most important,
all of them will know me.
I will forgive their evil ways.
I will not remember their sins anymore."

God called this covenant "new." So he has done away with the first one. And what is out of date and has been done away with will soon disappear.

⟡⟡⟡

The first covenant had rules for worship. It also had a sacred tent on earth. God showed his glory there. The priests entered it at regular times. But only the high priest went into the inner room. He went in only once a year. He never entered without taking blood with him. He offered the blood for himself. He also offered it for the sins the people had committed because they didn't know any better.

But Christ came to be the high priest of the good things already here now. When he came, he went through the greater and more perfect holy tent. He did not enter by spilling the blood of goats and calves. He entered the Most Holy Room by spilling his own blood. He did it once and for all time. In this way, he paid the price to set us free from sin forever.

Brothers and sisters, we are not afraid to enter the Most Holy Room. We enter boldly because of the blood of Jesus. So let us come near to God with a sincere heart. Let us come near boldly because of our faith. Our hearts have been sprinkled. Our minds have been cleansed from a sense of guilt. Our bodies have been washed with pure water. Let us hold firmly to the hope we claim to have. The God who promised is faithful. Let us consider how we can stir up one another to love. Let us help one another to do good works. And let us not give up meeting together. Instead, let us encourage one another with words of hope. Let us do this even more as you see Christ's return approaching.

Sometimes people spoke badly about you in front of others. Sometimes you were treated badly. At other times you stood side by side with people being treated like this. You suffered along with people in prison. When your property was taken from you, you accepted it with joy. You knew that God had given you better and more lasting things. So don't throw away your bold faith. It will bring you rich rewards.

॰෮ᏁᏁᎧ෮

Faith is being sure of what we hope for. It is being sure of what we do not see. That is what the people of long ago were praised for.

Abraham had faith. Abraham was past the time when he could have children. But many children came from that one man. They were as many as the stars in the sky. No one could count them.

Moses had faith. So he refused to be called the son of Pharaoh's daughter. He chose to be treated badly together with the people of God. Because of his faith, Moses left Egypt. It wasn't because he was afraid of the king's anger. He didn't let anything stop him. That's because he saw the God who can't be seen.

The people of Israel had faith. So they passed through the Red Sea. They went through it as if it were dry land.

Israel's army had faith. So the walls of Jericho fell down. It happened after they had marched around the city for seven days.

Rahab, the prostitute, had faith. So she welcomed the spies. That's why she wasn't killed with those who didn't obey God.

What more can I say? I don't have time to tell about all the others. I don't have time to talk about Gideon, Barak, Samson and Jephthah. I don't have time to tell about David and Samuel and the prophets. Because of their faith they took over kingdoms. They shut the mouths of lions. They put out great fires. Their weakness was turned to strength. Some were made fun of and even whipped. Some were held by chains. Some were put in prison. Some were killed with stones. Some were sawed in two. Some were killed by swords. They were poor. They were attacked. They were treated badly. The world was not worthy of them.

All these people were praised because they had faith. But none of them received what God had promised. That's because God had planned something better for us. So they would only be made perfect together with us.

A huge cloud of witnesses is all around us. So let us throw off everything that stands in our way. Let us throw off any sin that holds on to us so tightly. And let us keep on running the race marked out for us. Let us keep looking to Jesus. He is the one who started this journey of faith. And he is the one who completes the journey of faith.

You struggle against sin. But you have not yet fought to the point of spilling your blood.

Put up with hard times. God uses them to train you. No training seems pleasant at the time. In fact, it seems painful. But later on it produces a harvest of godliness and peace.

So put your hands to work. Strengthen your legs for the journey.

Keep on loving one another as brothers and sisters. Don't forget to welcome outsiders. Keep on remembering those in prison. Do this as if you were together with them in prison. And remember those who are treated badly as if you yourselves were suffering.

Remember your leaders. They spoke God's word to you. Think about the results of their way of life. Copy their faith. Jesus Christ is the same yesterday and today and forever.

Don't let all kinds of strange teachings lead you astray.

Don't forget to do good. Don't forget to share with others. God is pleased with those kinds of offerings.

Our Lord Jesus is the great Shepherd of the sheep. The God who gives peace brought him back from the dead. He did it because of the blood of the eternal covenant. Now may God supply you with everything good. Then you can do what he wants. May he do in us what is pleasing to him. We can do it only with the help of Jesus Christ. Give him glory for ever and ever. Amen.

remember what you read

1. What is something you noticed for the first time?

_____

_____

_____

_____

2. What questions did you have?

_____

_____

_____

_____

3. Was there anything that bothered you?

_____

_____

_____

_____

4. What did you learn about loving God?

_____

_____

_____

_____

5. What did you learn about loving others?

_____

_____

_____

_____

introduction to James

Jesus had many brothers. One of them was named James. After Jesus died and rose again, James became one the most important leaders in the community of Jesus-followers, also known as the church.

Many people looked up to James because he was very wise. He always gave good advice. At one point in his life, James decided to write down some of his best wisdom. He sent it to Jewish believers living all over the Roman Empire.

These writings are known as the book of James, and they're not like any other book in the New Testament. James is a collection of short sayings and teachings. Have you ever heard of the Old Testament book of Proverbs? Well, in some ways, James is a lot like Proverbs.

James has a way of asking important questions—questions that make you think about how you live. And that's what James is most interested in: how should we live out our faith in way that makes God happy?

As you read, you'll hear good advice about lots of things: treating people fairly, watching what you say, getting along with others, and caring for the poor. See how many "pearls of wisdom" you can remember from this short letter.

I, James, am writing this letter. I serve God and the Lord Jesus Christ.

I am sending this letter to you, the 12 tribes scattered among the nations.

Greetings.

My brothers and sisters, you will face all kinds of trouble. When you do, think of it as pure joy. Your faith will be tested. You know that when this happens it will produce in you the strength to continue. If any of you needs wisdom, you should ask God for it. He will give it to you. God gives freely to everyone and doesn't find fault. But when you ask, you must believe. You must not doubt. That's because a person who doubts is like a wave of the sea. The wind blows and tosses them around. They shouldn't expect to receive anything from the Lord. This kind of person can't make up their mind. They can never decide what to do.

ᑣᓍᓍᓂ

Blessed is the person who keeps on going when times are hard. After they have come through hard times, this person will receive a crown. The crown is life itself. The Lord has promised it to those who love him.

ᑣᓍᓍᓂ

My dear brothers and sisters, pay attention to what I say. Everyone should be quick to listen. But they should be slow to speak. They should be slow to get angry. Human anger doesn't produce the holy life God wants. So get rid of everything that is sinful. Get rid of the evil that is all around us. Don't be too proud to accept the word that is planted in you. It can save you.

ᑣᓍᓍᓂ

Suppose people think their beliefs and how they live are both right. But they don't control what they say. Then they are fooling themselves. Their beliefs and way of life are not worth anything at all. Here are the beliefs and way of life that God our Father accepts as pure and without fault. When widows are in trouble, take care of them. Do the same for children who have no parents. And don't let the world make you impure.

My brothers and sisters, you are believers in our glorious Lord Jesus Christ. So treat everyone the same. Suppose a man comes into your meeting wearing a gold ring and fine clothes. And suppose a poor man in dirty old clothes also comes in. Would you show special attention to the man wearing fine clothes? Would you say, "Here's a good seat for you"? Would you say to the poor man, "You stand there"? Or "Sit on the floor by my feet"? If you would, aren't you treating some people better than others? Aren't you like judges who have evil thoughts?

My dear brothers and sisters, listen to me. Hasn't God chosen those who are poor in the world's eyes to be rich in faith? Hasn't he chosen them to receive the kingdom? Hasn't he promised it to those who love him?

The royal law is found in Scripture. It says, "Love your neighbor as you love yourself." If you really keep this law, you are doing what is right. But you sin if you don't treat everyone the same.

Suppose a person claims to have faith but doesn't act on their faith. My brothers and sisters, can this kind of faith save them? Suppose a brother or a sister has no clothes or food. Suppose one of you says to them, "Go. I hope everything turns out fine for you. Keep warm. Eat well." And suppose you do nothing about what they really need. Then what good have you done? It is the same with faith. If it doesn't cause us to do something, it's dead.

So you see that a person is considered right with God by what they do. It doesn't happen only because they believe.

A person's body without their spirit is dead. In the same way, faith without good deeds is dead.

The tongue is a small part of a person's body. But it talks big. Think about how a small spark can set a big forest on fire. The tongue is also a fire. The tongue is the most evil part of the body. It makes the whole body impure.

People have tamed all kinds of wild animals, birds, reptiles and sea creatures. And they still tame them. But no one can tame the tongue. It is an evil thing that never rests. It is full of deadly poison.

With our tongues we praise our Lord and Father. With our tongues we curse people. Praise and cursing come out of the same mouth. My brothers and sisters, it shouldn't be this way.

⚬⚬⚬

Is anyone among you wise and understanding? That person should show it by living a good life. A wise person isn't proud when they do good deeds. But suppose your hearts are jealous and bitter. Suppose you are concerned only about getting ahead. Then don't brag about it. And don't say no to the truth. Wisdom like this doesn't come down from heaven. It belongs to the earth. It doesn't come from the Holy Spirit. It comes from the devil. Are you jealous? Are you concerned only about getting ahead? Then your life will be a mess. You will be doing all kinds of evil things.

But the wisdom that comes from heaven is pure. That's the most important thing about it. And that's not all. It also loves peace. It thinks about others. It obeys. It is full of mercy and good fruit. It is fair. It doesn't pretend to be what it is not.

⚬⚬⚬

Why do you fight and argue among yourselves? Isn't it because of your sinful desires? They fight within you. You want something, but you don't have it. So you kill. You want what others have, but you can't get what you want. So you argue and fight. You don't have what you want, because you don't ask God. When you do ask for something, you don't receive it. That's because you ask for the wrong reason. You want to spend your money on your sinful pleasures.

Stand up to the devil. He will run away from you. Come near to

God, and he will come near to you. Wash your hands, you sinners. Make your hearts pure, you who can't make up your minds. Be full of sorrow. Cry and weep. Change your laughter to mourning. Change your joy to sadness. Be humble in front of the Lord. And he will lift you up.

✺

Now listen, you who say, "Today or tomorrow we will go to this or that city. We will spend a year there. We will buy and sell and make money." You don't even know what will happen tomorrow. What is your life? It is a mist that appears for a little while. Then it disappears. Instead, you should say, "If it pleases the Lord, we will live and do this or that."

✺

Brothers and sisters, be patient until the Lord comes. See how the farmer waits for the land to produce its rich crop. See how patient the farmer is for the fall and spring rains. You too must be patient. You must remain strong. The Lord will soon come back. Brothers and sisters, don't find fault with one another. If you do, you will be judged. And the Judge is standing at the door!

✺

Is anyone among you in trouble? Then that person should pray. Is anyone among you happy? Then that person should sing songs of praise. Is anyone among you sick? Then that person should send for the elders of the church to pray over them. They should ask the elders to anoint them with olive oil in the name of the Lord. The prayer offered by those who have faith will make the sick person well. The Lord will heal them. If they have sinned, they will be forgiven. So confess your sins to one another. Pray for one another so that you might be healed. The prayer of a godly person is powerful. Things happen because of it.

Elijah was a human being, just as we are. He prayed hard that it wouldn't rain. And it didn't rain on the land for three and a half years. Then he prayed again. That time it rained. And the earth produced its crops.

༄

My brothers and sisters, suppose one of you wanders away from the truth. And suppose someone brings that person back. Then here is what I want you to remember. Anyone who keeps a sinner from going astray will save them from death. God will erase many sins by forgiving them.

remember what you read

1. What is something you noticed for the first time?

_____

_____

_____

_____

2. What questions did you have?

_____

_____

_____

_____

3. Was there anything that bothered you?

_____

_____

_____

_____

4. What did you learn about loving God?

_____

_____

_____

_____

5. What did you learn about loving others?

_____

_____

_____

_____

MARK, PART 1

introduction to Mark, part 1

When you give your life to Jesus, you have to be willing to suffer for him. No one knew this better than the believers who lived in Rome about 30 years after Jesus rose from the dead.

The Roman Empire was ruled by a man named Nero. Nero hated Christians. He had them tortured and killed. Some were thrown to the dogs. Some were crucified like Jesus. Others were burned alive. Legend has is that the apostle Peter, one of Jesus' disciples, was killed on Nero's orders.

The church in Rome needed encouragement. They needed to hear the story of Jesus once more. They needed an eyewitness account from someone who was actually there. They needed to know this story was worth dying for, if necessary.

Many believe that's why the gospel of Mark was written. It's likely this book contains the memories of Peter, who spent three years with Jesus. Peter trusted his friend and coworker Mark with the job of writing down this story, exactly as he remembered it.

Mark's gospel is fast-paced and action packed. In part one, people swarm to Jesus, all wanting to know the same thing: "Who is this man?"

As you read, ask yourself who you think he is and whether he's worth living—and dying—for.

෴

This is the beginning of the good news about Jesus the Messiah, the Son of God. Long ago Isaiah the prophet wrote,

"I will send my messenger ahead of you.
He will prepare your way."

And so John the Baptist appeared in the desert. He preached that people should be baptized and turn away from their sins. Then God would forgive them. All the people from the countryside of Judea went out to him. All the people from Jerusalem went too. When they admitted they had sinned, John baptized them in the Jordan River.

Here is what John was preaching. "After me, there is someone coming who is more powerful than I am. I baptize you with water. But he will baptize you with the Holy Spirit."

At that time Jesus came from Nazareth in Galilee. John baptized Jesus in the Jordan River. Jesus was coming up out of the water. Just then he saw heaven being torn open. Jesus saw the Holy Spirit coming down on him like a dove. A voice spoke to him from heaven. It said, "You are my Son, and I love you. I am very pleased with you."

At once the Holy Spirit sent Jesus out into the desert. He was in the desert 40 days. There Satan tempted him. The wild animals didn't harm Jesus. Angels took care of him.

∽👁👁👁∾

After John was put in prison, Jesus went into Galilee. He preached the good news of God. "The time has come," he said. "The kingdom of God has come near. Turn away from your sins and believe the good news!"

Jesus and those with him went to Capernaum. When the Sabbath day came, he went into the synagogue. There he began to teach. The people were amazed at his teaching. News about Jesus spread quickly all over Galilee.

A few days later, Jesus entered Capernaum again. So many people gathered that there was no room left. There was not even room outside the door. Four of those who came were carrying a man who could not walk. But they could not get him close to Jesus because of the crowd. So they made a hole by digging through the roof above Jesus. Then they lowered the man through it on a mat. Jesus saw their faith. So he said to the man, "Son, your sins are forgiven."

Some teachers of the law were sitting there. They were thinking, "Why is this fellow talking like that? He's saying a very evil thing! Only God can forgive sins!"

Right away Jesus knew what they were thinking. So he said to them, "Why are you thinking these things? Is it easier to say to this man, 'Your sins are forgiven'? Or to say, 'Get up, take your mat and walk'? But I want you to know that the Son of Man has authority on earth to forgive sins." So Jesus spoke to the man who could not walk. "I tell you," he said, "get up. Take your mat and go home." The man got up and took his mat. Then he walked away while everyone watched. All the people were amazed. They praised God and said, "We have never seen anything like this!"

Jesus went off to the Sea of Galilee with his disciples. A large crowd from Galilee followed. People heard about all that Jesus was doing. And many came to him.

ഗ്ല

Jesus went up on a mountainside. He called for certain people to come to him, and they came. He appointed the 12 disciples.

Simon was one of them. Jesus gave him the name Peter.
There were James, son of Zebedee, and his brother John. Jesus gave them the name Boanerges. Boanerges means Sons of Thunder.
There were also Andrew,
Philip,
Bartholomew,
Matthew,
Thomas,
and James, son of Alphaeus.
And there were Thaddaeus
and Simon the Zealot.
Judas Iscariot was one of them too. He was the one who was later going to hand Jesus over to his enemies.

Again Jesus began to teach by the Sea of Galilee. The crowd that gathered around him was very large.

When evening came, Jesus said to his disciples, "Let's go over to the other side of the lake." They left the crowd behind. And they took him along in a boat, just as he was. There were also other boats with him. A wild storm came up. Waves crashed over the boat. It was about to sink. Jesus was in the back, sleeping on a cushion. The disciples woke him up. They said, "Teacher! Don't you care if we drown?"

He got up and ordered the wind to stop. He said to the waves, "Quiet! Be still!" Then the wind died down. And it was completely calm.

He said to his disciples, "Why are you so afraid? Don't you have any faith at all yet?"

They were terrified. They asked each other, "Who is this? Even the wind and the waves obey him!"

Jesus went across the Sea of Galilee in a boat. It landed at the other side. There a large crowd gathered around him. Then a man named Jairus came. He was a synagogue leader. When he saw Jesus, he fell at his feet. He begged Jesus, "Please come. My little daughter is dying. Place your hands on her to heal her. Then she will live." So Jesus went with him.

A large group of people followed. They crowded around him. A woman was there who had a sickness that made her bleed. It had lasted for 12 years. She had suffered a great deal, even though she had gone to many doctors. She had spent all the money she had. But she was getting worse, not better. Then she heard about Jesus. She came up behind him in the crowd and touched his clothes. She thought, "I just need to touch his clothes. Then I will be healed." Right away her bleeding stopped. She felt in her body that her suffering was over.

At once Jesus knew that power had gone out from him. He turned around in the crowd. He asked, "Who touched my clothes?"

"You see the people," his disciples answered. "They are crowding against you."

But Jesus kept looking around. He wanted to see who had touched him. Then the woman came and fell at his feet. She was shaking with fear. But she told him the whole truth. He said to her, "Dear woman, your faith has healed you. Go in peace. You are free from your suffering."

While Jesus was still speaking, some people came from the house of Jairus. He was the synagogue leader. "Your daughter is dead," they said. "Why bother the teacher anymore?"

Jesus heard what they were saying. He told the synagogue leader, "Don't be afraid. Just believe."

They came to the home of the synagogue leader. There Jesus saw a lot of confusion. People were crying and sobbing loudly. He went inside. Then he said to them, "Why all this confusion and sobbing? The child is not dead. She is only sleeping." But they laughed at him.

He made them all go outside. He took only the child's father and mother and the disciples who were with him. And he went in where the child was. He took her by the hand. Then he said to her, "Little girl, I say to you, get up!" Right away she stood up and began to walk around. They were totally amazed at this. Jesus gave strict orders not to let anyone know what had happened. And he told them to give her something to eat.

Jesus left there and went to his hometown of Nazareth. His disciples went with him. When the Sabbath day came, he began to teach in the synagogue. Many who heard him were amazed.

"Where did this man get these things?" they asked.

Jesus placed his hands on a few sick people and healed them. But he could not do any other miracles there. He was amazed because they had no faith.

⌒⟋⟋⟋⌒

The apostles gathered around Jesus. But many people were coming and going. So they did not even have a chance to eat. Then Jesus said to his apostles, "Come with me by yourselves to a quiet place. You need to get some rest."

So they went away by themselves in a boat to a quiet place. But many people who saw them leaving recognized them. They ran from all the towns and got there ahead of them. When Jesus came ashore, he saw a large crowd. He felt deep concern for them. They were like sheep without a shepherd. So he began teaching them many things.

By that time it was late in the day. His disciples came to him. "There is nothing here," they said. "It's already very late. Send the people away. Then they can go to the nearby countryside and villages to buy something to eat."

But Jesus answered, "You give them something to eat."

They said to him, "That would take more than half a year's pay! Should we go and spend that much on bread? Are we supposed to feed them?"

"How many loaves do you have?" Jesus asked. "Go and see."

When they found out, they said, "Five loaves and two fish."

Jesus took the five loaves and the two fish. He looked up to heaven and gave thanks. He broke the loaves into pieces. Then he gave them to his disciples to pass around to the people. He also divided the two fish among them all. All of them ate and were satisfied. The disciples picked up 12 baskets of broken pieces of bread and fish. The number of men who had eaten was 5,000.

Right away Jesus made his disciples get into the boat. He had them go on ahead of him to Bethsaida.

Shortly before dawn, he went out to them. He walked on the lake. They thought he was a ghost, so they cried out. They all saw him and were terrified.

Right away Jesus said to them, "Be brave! It is I. Don't be afraid." Then he climbed into the boat with them. The wind died down. And they were completely amazed.

Jesus and his disciples came to Bethsaida. Some people brought a blind man to him. They begged Jesus to touch him. He took the blind man by the hand. Then he led him outside the village. He spit on the man's eyes and placed his hands on him. "Do you see anything?" Jesus asked.

The man looked up. He said, "I see people. They look like trees walking around."

Once more Jesus put his hands on the man's eyes. Then his eyes were opened so that he could see again. He saw everything clearly. Jesus sent him home. He told him, "Don't even go into the village."

Jesus and his disciples went on to the villages around Caesarea Philippi. On the way he asked them, "Who do people say I am?" They replied, "Some say John the Baptist. Others say Elijah. Still others say one of the prophets."

"But what about you?" he asked. "Who do you say I am?"

Peter answered, "You are the Messiah."

Jesus warned them not to tell anyone about him.

remember what you read

1. What is something you noticed for the first time?

_____

_____

_____

_____

2. What questions did you have?

_____

_____

_____

_____

3. Was there anything that bothered you?

_____

_____

_____

_____

4. What did you learn about loving God?

_____

_____

_____

_____

5. What did you learn about loving others?

_____

_____

_____

_____

introduction to Mark, part 2

Mark's story of Jesus is like a two-part movie. In part one, Jesus did some amazing things and left everyone— including his own followers—scratching their heads, wondering who he is.

In part two, the conflict between Jesus and the religious leaders kicks into high gear. Mark's gospel ends about as suddenly as it begins, with plenty of action packed in between.

Jesus called the crowd to him along with his disciples. He said, "Whoever wants to be my disciple must say no to themselves. They must pick up their cross and follow me. Whoever wants to save their life will lose it. But whoever loses their life for me and for the good news will save it. What good is it if someone gains the whole world but loses their soul? Or what can anyone trade for their soul?"

Jesus and his disciples came to a house in Capernaum. There he asked them, "What were you arguing about on the road?" But they kept quiet. On the way, they had argued about which one of them was the most important person.

Jesus sat down and called for the 12 disciples to come to him. Then he said, "Anyone who wants to be first must be the very last. They must be the servant of everyone."

Jesus took a little child and had the child stand among them. Then he took the child in his arms. He said to them, "Anyone who welcomes one of these little children in my name welcomes me. And anyone who welcomes me also welcomes the one who sent me."

People were bringing little children to Jesus. They wanted him to place his hands on them to bless them. But the disciples told them to stop. When Jesus saw this, he was angry. He said to his disciples, "Let the little children come to me. Don't keep them away. God's kingdom belongs to people like them. What I'm about to tell you is true. Anyone who will not receive God's kingdom like a little child will never enter it." Then he took the children in his arms. He placed his hands on them to bless them.

᳁ᳩᳩᳩᳩ᳁

When Jesus reached Jerusalem, he entered the temple courtyard. He began to drive out those who were buying and selling there. He turned over the tables of the people who were exchanging money. He also turned over the benches of those who were selling doves. He would not allow anyone to carry items for sale through the temple courtyard. Then he taught them. He told them, "It is written that the Lord said, 'My house will be called a house where people from all nations can pray.' But you have made it a 'den for robbers.'"

The chief priests and the teachers of the law heard about this. They began looking for a way to kill Jesus.

Judas Iscariot was one of the 12 disciples. He went to the chief priests to hand Jesus over to them. They were delighted to hear that he would do this. They promised to give Judas money. So he watched for the right time to hand Jesus over to them.

᳁ᳩᳩᳩᳩ᳁

It was the first day of the Feast of Unleavened Bread. That was the time to sacrifice the Passover lamb.

When evening came, Jesus arrived with the 12 disciples.

While they were eating, Jesus took bread. He gave thanks and broke it. He handed it to his disciples and said, "Take it. This is my body."

Then he took a cup. He gave thanks and handed it to them. All of them drank from it.

"This is my blood of the covenant," he said to them. "It is poured out for many."

Then they sang a hymn and went out to the Mount of Olives.

"You will all turn away," Jesus told the disciples.

Peter said, "All the others may turn away. But I will not."

"What I'm about to tell you is true," Jesus answered. "It will happen today, in fact tonight. Before the rooster crows twice, you yourself will say three times that you don't know me."

✿✿✿

Jesus and his disciples went to a place called Gethsemane. Jesus said to them, "Sit here while I pray." He took Peter, James and John along with him. He began to be very upset and troubled. "My soul is very sad. I feel close to death," he said to them. "Stay here. Keep watch."

He went a little farther. Then he fell to the ground. He prayed that, if possible, the hour might pass by him.

Then he returned to his disciples and found them sleeping. "Simon," he said to Peter, "are you asleep? Couldn't you keep watch for one hour?"

Once more Jesus went away and prayed the same thing. Then he came back. Again he found them sleeping.

Jesus returned the third time. He said to them, "Are you still sleeping and resting? Enough! The hour has come. Look! The Son of Man is about to be handed over to sinners."

Just as Jesus was speaking, Judas appeared. He was one of the 12 disciples. A crowd was with him. They were carrying swords and clubs. The chief priests, the teachers of the law, and the elders had sent them.

Judas, who was going to hand Jesus over, had arranged a signal with them. "The one I kiss is the man," he said. "Arrest him and have the guards lead him away." So Judas went to Jesus at once. Judas said, "Rabbi!" And he kissed Jesus. The men grabbed Jesus and arrested him.

"Am I leading a band of armed men against you?" asked Jesus. "Do you have to come out with swords and clubs to capture me?" Then everyone left him and ran away.

༄

The crowd took Jesus to the high priest. All the chief priests, the elders, and the teachers of the law came together.

Many witnesses lied about him.

"We heard him say, 'I will destroy this temple made by human hands. In three days I will build another temple, not made by human hands.'" But what they said did not agree.

Then the high priest stood up in front of them. He asked Jesus, "Aren't you going to answer? What are these charges these men are bringing against you?" But Jesus remained silent. He gave no answer.

Again the high priest asked him, "Are you the Messiah? Are you the Son of the Blessed One?"

"I am," said Jesus. "And you will see the Son of Man sitting at the right hand of the Mighty One. You will see the Son of Man coming on the clouds of heaven."

The high priest tore his clothes. "Why do we need any more witnesses?" he asked. "You have heard him say a very evil thing against God. What do you think?"

They all found him guilty and said he must die.

༄

Peter was below in the courtyard. One of the high priest's female servants came by. When she saw Peter warming himself, she looked closely at him.

"You also were with Jesus, that Nazarene," she said.

But Peter said he had not been with him. He went out to the entrance to the courtyard.

The servant saw him there. She said again to those standing around, "This fellow is one of them." Again he said he was not.

After a little while, those standing nearby said to Peter, "You must be one of them. You are from Galilee."

Then Peter began to curse. He said to them, "I don't know this man you're talking about!"

Right away the rooster crowed the second time. Then Peter remembered what Jesus had spoken to him. Peter broke down and cried.

It was very early in the morning. The chief priests, with the elders, the teachers of the law, and the whole Sanhedrin, made their plans. So they tied Jesus up and led him away. Then they handed him over to Pilate.

"Are you the king of the Jews?" asked Pilate.

"You have said so," Jesus replied.

The chief priests brought many charges against him. So Pilate asked him again, "Aren't you going to answer? See how many things they charge you with."

But Jesus still did not reply. Pilate was amazed.

"Do you want me to let the king of the Jews go free?" asked Pilate. But the chief priests stirred up the crowd.

"Then what should I do with the one you call the king of the Jews?" Pilate asked them.

"Crucify him!" the crowd shouted.

Pilate wanted to satisfy the crowd. He ordered that Jesus be whipped. Then he handed him over to be nailed to a cross.

The soldiers led Jesus away into the palace. The soldiers put a purple robe on Jesus. Then they twisted thorns together to make a crown. They placed it on his head. Again and again they hit him on the head with a stick. They spit on him. After they had made fun of him, they took off the purple robe. They put his own clothes back on him. Then they led him out to nail him to a cross.

A man named Simon was passing by. He was from Cyrene. He was the father of Alexander and Rufus. Simon was on his way in from the country. The soldiers forced him to carry the cross.

They brought Jesus to the place called Golgotha. They nailed him to the cross.

It was nine o'clock in the morning when they crucified him.

Those who passed by shouted at Jesus and made fun of him. In the same way the chief priests and the teachers of the law made fun of him among themselves. "He saved others," they said. "But he can't save himself!"

At noon, darkness covered the whole land. It lasted three hours. At three o'clock in the afternoon Jesus cried out in a loud voice, "My God, my God, why have you deserted me?"

Some of those standing nearby heard Jesus cry out. They said, "Listen! He's calling for Elijah."

Someone ran and filled a sponge with wine vinegar. He put it on a stick. He offered it to Jesus to drink. "Leave him alone," he said. "Let's see if Elijah comes to take him down."

With a loud cry, Jesus took his last breath.

A Roman commander was standing there in front of Jesus. He saw how Jesus died. Then he said, "This man was surely the Son of God!"

Not very far away, some women were watching. Mary Magdalene was among them. Mary, the mother of the younger James and of Joseph, was also there. So was Salome. In Galilee these women had followed Jesus. They had taken care of his needs.

⟡

As evening approached, Joseph went boldly to Pilate and asked for Jesus' body. Joseph was from the town of Arimathea. He was a leading member of the Jewish Council. He was waiting for God's kingdom.

Then Joseph bought some linen cloth. He took down the body and wrapped it in the linen. He put it in a tomb cut out of rock. Then he rolled a stone against the entrance to the tomb. Mary Magdalene and Mary the mother of Joseph saw where Jesus' body had been placed.

⟡

Mary Magdalene, Mary the mother of James, and Salome bought spices. They were going to use them for Jesus' body. Very early on the first day of the week, they were on their way to the tomb. It was just after sunrise. They asked each other, "Who will roll the stone away from the entrance to the tomb?"

Then they looked up and saw that the stone had been rolled away. The stone was very large. They entered the tomb. As they did, they saw a young man dressed in a white robe. He was sitting on the right side. They were alarmed.

"Don't be alarmed," he said. "You are looking for Jesus the Nazarene, who was crucified. But he has risen! He is not here! Go! Tell his disciples and Peter, 'He is going ahead of you into Galilee. There you will see him.'"

The women were shaking and confused. They went out and ran away from the tomb. They said nothing to anyone, because they were afraid.

remember what you read

1. What is something you noticed for the first time?

_____

_____

_____

_____

2. What questions did you have?

_____

_____

_____

_____

3. Was there anything that bothered you?

_____

_____

_____

_____

4. What did you learn about loving God?

_____

_____

_____

_____

5. What did you learn about loving others?

_____

_____

_____

_____

I PETER

introduction to 1 Peter

Peter was one of the twelve disciples. You may remember him as the one who denied Jesus three times the night before he was killed.

But after Jesus rose from the dead, Peter became an important leader in the church. He spent the last years of his life in Rome, helping believers who lived there.

But Peter also wanted to help Christians who lived far away, who were suffering because of their faith. So he wrote them a letter.

In his letter, Peter told them to be holy, which means "set apart." Instead of blending in, they were supposed to stand out. Why? Because according to Peter, they were a "holy nation." A kingdom of "royal priests."

A priest is someone who shows the way to God. "The world is watching," Peter said. "Let's show them what God is like by how we live—by doing good and by loving each other. Then they'll have no choice but to give glory to God."

As you read Peter's letter, think about how you can use your life to show others what God is like.

I, Peter, am writing this letter. I am an apostle of Jesus Christ.

I am sending this letter to you, God's chosen people. You are people who have had to wander in the world. You are scattered all over. You have been chosen in keeping with what God the Father had planned. That happened through the Spirit's work to make you pure and holy. God chose you so that you might obey Jesus

Christ. God wanted you to be in a covenant relationship with him. He established this relationship by the blood of Christ.

May more and more grace and peace be given to you.

❧

Your salvation is going to be completed. Because you know this, you have great joy. You have joy even though you may have had to suffer for a little while. Your troubles have come in order to prove that your faith is real. Your faith is worth more than gold.

So be watchful, and control yourselves completely. In this way, put your hope in the grace that lies ahead. This grace will be brought to you when Jesus Christ returns. The God who chose you is holy. So you should be holy in all that you do. It is written, "Be holy, because I am holy."

You know that you were not bought with things that can pass away, like silver or gold. Instead, you were bought with the priceless blood of Christ. He is a perfect lamb. He doesn't have any flaws at all. He was chosen before God created the world. But he came into the world for your sake in these last days. Because of what Christ has done, you believe in God. It was God who raised him from the dead. And it was God who gave him glory. So your faith and hope are in God.

You have made yourselves pure by obeying the truth. So you have an honest and true love for each other. So love one another deeply, from your hearts. You have been born again by means of the living word of God. His word lasts forever. You were not born again from a seed that will die. You were born from a seed that can't die.

So get rid of every kind of evil, and stop telling lies. Don't pretend to be something you are not. Stop wanting what others have, and don't speak against one another. Like newborn babies, you should long for the pure milk of God's word. It will help you grow up as believers. You can do this now that you have tasted how good the Lord is.

❧

God chose you to be his people. You are royal priests. You are a holy nation. You are God's special treasure. You are all these things so that you can give him praise. God brought you out of darkness into his wonderful light. Once you were not a people. But now you are the people of God. Once you had not received mercy. But now you have received mercy.

Dear friends, you are outsiders and those who wander in this world. So I'm asking you not to give in to your sinful desires. They fight against your soul. People who don't believe might say you are doing wrong. But lead good lives among them. Then they will see your good deeds. And they will give glory to God on the day he comes to judge.

Live as free people. But don't use your freedom to cover up evil. Live as people who are God's slaves. Show proper respect to everyone. Love the family of believers. Have respect for God.

Finally, I want all of you to agree with one another. Be understanding. Love one another. Be kind and tender. Be humble. Don't pay back evil with evil. Don't pay back unkind words with unkind words. Instead, pay back evil with kind words.

Who is going to hurt you if you really want to do good? But suppose you do suffer for doing what is right. Even then you will be blessed. But make sure that in your hearts you honor Christ as Lord. Always be ready to give an answer to anyone who asks you about the hope you have. Be ready to give the reason for it. But do it gently and with respect.

The end of all things is near. So be watchful and control yourselves. Then you may pray. Most of all, love one another deeply. Love erases many sins by forgiving them. Welcome others into your homes without complaining. God's gifts of grace come in many forms. Each of you has received a gift in order to serve others. You should use it faithfully. If anyone speaks, they should do it as one speaking God's words. If anyone serves, they should do it with the strength God provides. Then in all things God will be praised through Jesus Christ.

Dear friends, don't be surprised by the terrible things happening to you. The trouble you are having has come to test you. So don't feel as if something strange were happening to you. Instead, be joyful that you are taking part in Christ's sufferings. Then you will have even more joy when Christ returns in glory. Suppose people say bad things about you because you believe in Christ. Then you are blessed, because God's Spirit rests on you. He is the Spirit of glory. If you suffer, it shouldn't be because you are a murderer. It shouldn't be because you are a thief or someone who does evil things. It shouldn't be because you interfere with other people's business. But suppose you suffer for being a Christian. Then don't be ashamed. Instead, praise God because you are known by the name of Christ. It is time for judgment to begin with the household of God. And since it begins with us, what will happen to people who don't obey God's good news? Scripture says,

"Suppose it is hard for godly people to be saved.
Then what will happen to ungodly people and sinners?"

Here is what people who suffer because of God's plan should do. They should commit themselves to their faithful Creator. And they should continue to do good.

⟳

I'm speaking to the elders among you. Be shepherds of God's flock, the believers under your care. Watch over them, though not because you have to. Instead, do it because you want to. That's what God wants you to do. Don't do it because you want to get money in dishonest ways. Do it because you really want to serve. Don't act as if you were a ruler over those under your care. Instead, be examples to the flock. The Chief Shepherd will come again. Then you will receive the crown of glory. It is a crown that will never fade away.

In the same way, I'm speaking to you who are younger. Follow the lead of those who are older. All of you, put on a spirit free of pride toward one another. Put it on as if it were your clothes. Do this because Scripture says,

"God opposes those who are proud.
But he gives grace to those who are humble."

So make yourselves humble. Put yourselves under God's mighty hand. Then he will honor you at the right time. Turn all your worries over to him. He cares about you.

Be watchful and control yourselves. Your enemy the devil is like a roaring lion. He prowls around looking for someone to swallow up. Stand up to him. Remain strong in what you believe. You know that you are not alone in your suffering. The family of believers throughout the world is going through the same thing.

God always gives you all the grace you need. So you will only have to suffer for a little while. Then God himself will build you up again. He will make you strong and steady. And he has chosen you to share in his eternal glory because you belong to Christ. Give him the power for ever and ever. Amen.

∽∾

I consider Silas to be a faithful brother. With his help I have written you this short letter. I have written it to encourage you. And I have written to speak the truth about the true grace of God. Remain strong in it.

The members of the church in Babylon send you their greetings. They were chosen together with you. Mark, my son in the faith, also sends you his greetings.

Greet each other with a kiss of friendship.

May God give peace to all of you who believe in Christ.

remember what you read

1. What is something you noticed for the first time?

_____

_____

_____

_____

2. What questions did you have?

_____

_____

_____

_____

3. Was there anything that bothered you?

_____

_____

_____

_____

4. What did you learn about loving God?

_____

_____

_____

_____

5. What did you learn about loving others?

_____

_____

_____

_____

2 PETER, JUDE

introduction to 2 Peter

Peter was an important leader of the church in Rome. But he was arrested and put in jail by the emperor, Nero. (You might recognize this name from a few readings back, when we introduced Mark's story about Jesus.)

Nero hated Christians. Paul knew there was little chance of getting out alive. So he wrote one last letter to the believers he had written before. He wanted to make sure they knew that everything they'd been told about Jesus was true. It wasn't just a bunch of made-up stories.

Peter also had to deal with some false teachers who were telling people that Jesus was never going to come back. Lots of people were wondering why it was taking so long for Jesus to return as he had promised. Peter explains that it's because God is patient. He doesn't want anyone to be destroyed. He wants everyone to have a chance to turn away from their sin and trust him.

But one thing is sure: Jesus is coming back. We can look forward to spending forever with him in a new heaven and a new earth. Because of this, Peter says we should live for God now so we can be happy when he comes back.

∽͡ᚹᚹ͡ᚹ᠆

I, Simon Peter, am writing this letter. I serve Jesus Christ. I am his apostle.

May more and more grace and peace be given to you. May they come to you as you learn more about God and about Jesus our Lord.

God's power has given us everything we need to lead a godly life. All of this has come to us because we know the God who chose us. He chose us because of his own glory and goodness.

So you should try very hard to add goodness to your faith. To goodness, add knowledge. To knowledge, add the ability to control yourselves. To the ability to control yourselves, add the strength to keep going. To the strength to keep going, add godliness. To godliness, add kindness for one another. And to kindness for one another, add love.

My brothers and sisters, try very hard to show that God has appointed you to be saved. Try hard to show that he has chosen you. If you do everything I have just said, you will never trip and fall. You will receive a rich welcome into the kingdom that lasts forever. It is the kingdom of our Lord and Savior Jesus Christ.

So I will always remind you of these things. I'll do it even though you know them. I'll do it even though you now have deep roots in the truth. I hope that you will always be able to remember these things after I'm gone. I will try very hard to see that you do.

We told you about the time our Lord Jesus Christ came with power. But we didn't make up clever stories when we told you about it. With our own eyes we saw him in all his majesty.

〜〜

But there were also false prophets among the people. In the same way there will be false teachers among you. In secret they will bring in teachings that will destroy you. They will even turn against the Lord and Master who died to pay for their sins. So they will quickly destroy themselves. Many people will follow their lead. These people will do the same evil things the false teachers do. They will cause people to think badly about the way of truth. These teachers are never satisfied. They want to get something out of you. So they make up stories to take advantage of you. They have been under a sentence of death for a long time. The God who will destroy them has not been sleeping. They will be paid back with harm for the harm they have done.

These people are like springs without water. They are like mists driven by a storm. The blackest darkness is reserved for them. They speak empty, bragging words. They make their appeal to the evil desires that come from sin's power. They tempt new believers who are just escaping from the company of sinful people. They promise to give freedom to these new believers. But they themselves are slaves to sinful living. That's because "people are slaves to anything that controls them." They may have escaped the sin of the world. They may have come to know our Lord and Savior Jesus Christ. But what if they are once again caught up in sin? And what if it has become their master? Then they are worse off at the end than they were at the beginning. What the proverbs say about them is true. "A dog returns to where it has thrown up." And, "A pig that is washed goes back to rolling in the mud."

Dear friends, this is now my second letter to you. I have written both of them as reminders. I want to encourage you to think in a way that is pure.

Most of all, here is what you must understand. In the last days people will make fun of the truth. They will laugh at it. They will follow their own evil desires. They will say, "Where is this 'return' he promised? By God's word the heavens and earth of today are being reserved for fire. They are being kept for the day when God will judge. Then ungodly people will be destroyed.

Dear friends, here is one thing you must not forget. With the Lord a day is like a thousand years. And a thousand years are like a day. The Lord is not slow to keep his promise. He is not slow in the way some people understand it. Instead, he is patient with you. He doesn't want anyone to be destroyed. Instead, he wants all people to turn away from their sins.

But the day of the Lord will come like a thief. The heavens will disappear with a roar. Fire will destroy everything in them. God will judge the earth and everything done in it.

So everything will be destroyed in this way. And what kind of people should you be? You should lead holy and godly lives. Live like this as you look forward to the day of God. Living like this will make the day come more quickly. On that day fire will destroy the heavens. Its heat will melt everything in them. But we are looking forward to a new heaven and a new earth. Godliness will live there. All this is in keeping with God's promise.

Dear friends, I know you are looking forward to this. So try your best to be found pure and without blame. Be at peace with God. Remember that while our Lord is waiting patiently to return, people are being saved.

Grow in the grace and knowledge of our Lord and Savior Jesus Christ.

Glory belongs to him both now and forever. Amen.

introduction to Jude

Jesus has several brothers. One of them was Jude. We don't know very much about Jude, but we do know he wrote a letter to some followers of Jesus, warning them about false teachers who were turning people away from God. These teachers rejected authority and did evil things. They claimed to be messengers of God, but Jude warned that they did not have the Holy Spirit.

As you read, see if you notice anything familiar about Jude's short letter. If you do, that's because it's very similar to Peter's second letter, which you read just a few moments ago.

Jude finishes his letter by encouraging everyone to stand firm and to help those who are struggling to follow Jesus. He says that as we help others, God will help us.

I, Jude, am writing this letter. I serve Jesus Christ. I am a brother of James.

I am sending this letter to you who have been chosen by God. You are loved by God the Father. You are kept safe for Jesus Christ.

May more and more mercy, peace and love be given to you.

Dear friends, I really wanted to write to you about the salvation we share. But now I feel I should write and ask you to stand up for the faith. God's holy people were trusted with it once and for all time. Certain people have secretly slipped in among you. Long ago it was written that they would be judged. They are ungodly people. They say no to Jesus Christ, our only Lord and King.

They don't accept authority. And they say evil things against heavenly beings.

They are shepherds who feed only themselves. They are like clouds without rain. They are blown along by the wind. They are like trees in the fall. Since they have no fruit, they are pulled out of the ground. So they die twice. They are like wild waves of the sea. Their shame rises up like foam. They are like falling stars. God has reserved a place of very black darkness for them forever.

Dear friends, remember what the apostles of our Lord Jesus Christ said would happen. They told you, "In the last days, some people will make fun of the truth. They will follow their own ungodly desires." They are the people who separate you from one another. They do only what comes naturally. They are not led by the Holy Spirit.

But you, dear friends, build yourselves up in your most holy faith. Let the Holy Spirit guide and help you when you pray. And by doing these things, remain in God's love as you wait.

Show mercy to those who doubt. Save others by pulling them out of the fire. To others, show mercy mixed with fear of sin. Hate even the clothes that are stained by the sins of those who wear them.

Give praise to the God who is able to keep you from falling into sin. He will bring you into his heavenly glory without any fault. He will bring you there with great joy. Amen.

remember what you read

1. What is something you noticed for the first time?

_____

_____

_____

_____

2. What questions did you have?

_____

_____

_____

_____

3. Was there anything that bothered you?

_____

_____

_____

_____

4. What did you learn about loving God?

_____

_____

_____

_____

5. What did you learn about loving others?

_____

_____

_____

_____

The Word was with God

introduction to John, part 1

Have you ever heard the story of creation? If so, do you remember how it begins? If you said, "In the beginning," then you guessed right!

Many years ago, a disciple named John decided to write about Jesus. John was one of his closest followers, and he wanted the world to know and believe in Jesus.

To begin, John uses the first three words of the creation story: "In the beginning." Why? Because Jesus marks a brand new starting point—a new creation. Jesus, who John sometimes calls "the Word," was there all the way back at creation. And he is here now, creating new life for those who believe in him!

In the first part of his book, John mentions seven signs or miracles that Jesus did to prove he was the true Son of God. In today's reading, we'll hear the first five of these signs. See if you can name them all after reading.

After a brief introduction, John picks up his story with another John: John the Baptist, who points the way to Jesus.

In the beginning, the Word was already there. The Word was with God, and the Word was God. He was with God in the beginning. All things were made through him. Nothing that has been made was made without him.

The Word was in the world. And the world was made through him. But the world did not recognize him. He came to what was his own. But his own people did not accept him. Some people did accept him and did believe in his name. He gave them the right to become children of God.

The Word became a human being. He made his home with us. We have seen his glory. It is the glory of the One and Only, who came from the Father. And the Word was full of grace and truth.

⟐

The Jewish leaders in Jerusalem sent priests and Levites to ask John who he was.

He said, "I am not the Messiah. I'm the messenger who is calling out in the desert, 'Make the way for the Lord straight.'"

This all happened at Bethany on the other side of the Jordan River. That was where John was baptizing.

The next day John saw Jesus coming toward him. John said, "Look! The Lamb of God! He takes away the sin of the world!

⟐

On the third day there was a wedding. It took place at Cana in Galilee. Jesus' mother was there. Jesus and his disciples had also been invited to the wedding. When the wine was gone, Jesus' mother said to him, "They have no more wine."

Six stone water jars stood nearby. Jesus said to the servants, "Fill the jars with water." So they filled them to the top.

Then he told them, "Now dip some out. Take it to the person in charge of the dinner."

They did what he said. The person in charge tasted the water that had been turned into wine. He didn't realize where it had come from. But the servants who had brought the water knew. Then the person in charge called the groom to one side. He said to him, "Everyone brings out the best wine first. They bring out the cheaper wine after the guests have had too much to drink. But you have saved the best until now."

What Jesus did here in Cana in Galilee was the first of his signs. Jesus showed his glory by doing this sign. And his disciples believed in him.

∽๛〜

It was almost time for the Jewish Passover Feast. So Jesus went up to Jerusalem. In the temple courtyard he found people selling cattle, sheep and doves. Others were sitting at tables exchanging money. So Jesus made a whip out of ropes. He chased all the sheep and cattle from the temple courtyard. He scattered the coins of the people exchanging money. And he turned over their tables. He told those who were selling doves, "Get these out of here! Stop turning my Father's house into a market!"

∽๛〜

There was a Pharisee named Nicodemus. He was one of the Jewish rulers. He came to Jesus at night and said, "Rabbi, we know that you are a teacher who has come from God. We know that God is with you. If he weren't, you couldn't do the signs you are doing."

Jesus replied, "What I'm about to tell you is true. No one can see God's kingdom unless they are born again."

"How can someone be born when they are old?" Nicodemus asked. "They can't go back inside their mother! They can't be born a second time!"

Jesus answered, "No one can enter God's kingdom unless they are born with water and the Holy Spirit. People give birth to people. But the Spirit gives birth to spirit. You should not be surprised when I say, 'You must all be born again.'"

God so loved the world that he gave his one and only Son. Anyone who believes in him will not die but will have eternal life. God did not send his Son into the world to judge the world. He sent his Son to save the world through him. Anyone who believes in him is not judged. But anyone who does not believe is judged already. They have not believed in the name of God's one and only Son.

∽๛〜

Once more, Jesus visited Cana in Galilee. Cana is where he had turned the water into wine. A royal official was there. His son was sick in bed at Capernaum. The official heard that Jesus had arrived in Galilee from Judea. So he went to Jesus and begged him to come and heal his son. The boy was close to death.

Jesus told him, "You people will never believe unless you see signs and wonders."

The royal official said, "Sir, come down before my child dies."

"Go," Jesus replied. "Your son will live."

The man believed what Jesus said, and so he left. While he was still on his way home, his slaves met him. They gave him the news that his boy was living. He asked what time his son got better. They said to him, "Yesterday, at one o'clock in the afternoon, the fever left him."

Then the father realized what had happened. That was the exact time Jesus had said to him, "Your son will live." So he and his whole family became believers.

This was the second sign that Jesus did after coming from Judea to Galilee.

⌒ᘓᘓᖚ

Some time later, Jesus went up to Jerusalem for one of the Jewish feasts. In Jerusalem near the Sheep Gate is a pool. Here a great number of disabled people used to lie down. Among them were those who were blind, those who could not walk, and those who could hardly move. One person was there who had not been able to walk for 38 years. Jesus saw him lying there. He knew that the man had been in that condition for a long time. So he asked him, "Do you want to get well?"

"Sir," the disabled man replied, "I have no one to help me into the pool when an angel stirs up the water. I try to get in, but someone else always goes down ahead of me."

Then Jesus said to him, "Get up! Pick up your mat and walk." The man was healed right away. He picked up his mat and walked.

⌒ᘓᘓᖚ

Some time after this, Jesus crossed over to the other side of the Sea of Galilee. It is also called the Sea of Tiberias. A large crowd of people followed him. They had seen the signs he had done by healing sick people.

Jesus looked up and saw a large crowd coming toward him. So he said to Philip, "Where can we buy bread for these people to eat?" He asked this only to test Philip. He already knew what he was going to do.

Philip answered him, "Suppose we were able to buy enough bread for each person to have just a bite. That would take more than half a year's pay!"

Another of his disciples spoke up. It was Andrew, Simon Peter's brother. He said, "Here is a boy with five small loaves of barley bread. He also has two small fish. But how far will that go in such a large crowd?"

Jesus said, "Have the people sit down." There was plenty of grass in that place, and they sat down. About 5,000 men were there. Then Jesus took the loaves and gave thanks. He handed out the bread to those who were seated. He gave them as much as they wanted. And he did the same with the fish.

When all of them had enough to eat, Jesus spoke to his disciples. "Gather the leftover pieces," he said. "Don't waste anything." So they gathered what was left over from the five barley loaves. They filled 12 baskets with the pieces left by those who had eaten.

⟨∽℺℺∿⟩

When evening came, Jesus' disciples went down to the Sea of Galilee. There they got into a boat and headed across the lake toward Capernaum. By now it was dark. Jesus had not yet joined them. A strong wind was blowing, and the water became rough. They rowed about three or four miles. Then they saw Jesus coming toward the boat. He was walking on the water. They were frightened. But he said to them, "It is I. Don't be afraid." Then they agreed to take him into the boat. Right away the boat reached the shore where they were heading.

⟨∽℺℺∿⟩

The next day the crowd realized that Jesus and his disciples were not there. So they got into boats and went to Capernaum to look for Jesus.

They found him on the other side of the lake. They asked him, "Rabbi, when did you get here?"

Jesus answered, "What I'm about to tell you is true. You are not looking for me because you saw the signs I did. You are looking for me because you ate the loaves until you were full. Do not work for food that spoils. Work for food that lasts forever. That is the food the Son of Man will give you. For God the Father has put his seal of approval on him."

Then they asked him, "What does God want from us? What works does he want us to do?"

Jesus answered, "God's work is to believe in the one he has sent."

So they asked him, "What sign will you give us? What will you do so we can see it and believe you?"

Jesus said to them, "What I'm about to tell you is true. The bread of God is the bread that comes down from heaven. He gives life to the world."

"Sir," they said, "always give us this bread."

Then Jesus said, "I am the bread of life. Whoever comes to me will never go hungry. But it is just as I told you. You have seen me, and you still do not believe."

Then the Jews there began to complain about Jesus. They said, "Isn't this Jesus, the son of Joseph? Don't we know his father and mother? How can he now say, 'I came down from heaven'?"

"Stop complaining among yourselves," Jesus answered. "I am the living bread that came down from heaven. Everyone who eats some of this bread will live forever. This bread is my body. I will give it for the life of the world."

Jesus' disciples heard this. Many of them said, "This is a hard teaching. Who can accept it?"

From this time on, many of his disciples turned back. They no longer followed him.

"You don't want to leave also, do you?" Jesus asked the 12 disciples.

Simon Peter answered him, "Lord, who can we go to? You have the words of eternal life. We have come to believe and to know that you are the Holy One of God."

remember what you read

1. What is something you noticed for the first time?

_____

_____

_____

_____

2. What questions did you have?

_____

_____

_____

_____

3. Was there anything that bothered you?

_____

_____

_____

_____

4. What did you learn about loving God?

_____

_____

_____

_____

5. What did you learn about loving others?

_____

_____

_____

_____

introduction to John, part 2

In his story about Jesus, John mentions seven miracles or signs Jesus did to prove he came from God. We heard about five of these signs in yesterday's reading. But two of the most incredible miracles are still to come.

Not everyone was happy about this display of power, though. Some of the Jewish leaders see Jesus as a threat, and they'll do anything to stop him.

After this, Jesus went around in Galilee. He didn't want to travel around in Judea. That was because the Jewish leaders there were looking for a way to kill him. The Jewish Feast of Booths was near.

Jesus did nothing until halfway through the feast. Then he went up to the temple courtyard and began to teach. The Jews there were amazed. They asked, "How did this man learn so much without being taught?"

Jesus answered, "What I teach is not my own. It comes from the one who sent me."

It was the last and most important day of the feast. Jesus stood up and spoke in a loud voice. He said, "Let anyone who is thirsty come to me and drink. Does anyone believe in me? Then, just as Scripture says, rivers of living water will flow from inside them."

The people heard his words. Some of them said, "This man must be the Prophet we've been expecting."

Others said, "He is the Messiah."

Still others asked, "How can the Messiah come from Galilee? Doesn't Scripture say that the Messiah will come from the family line of David? Doesn't it say that he will come from Bethlehem, the town where David lived?" So the people did not agree about who Jesus was.

Jesus spoke to the people again. He said, "I am the light of the world. Anyone who follows me will never walk in darkness. They will have that light. They will have life."

✺

As Jesus went along, he saw a man who was blind. He had been blind since he was born. Jesus' disciples asked him, "Rabbi, who sinned? Was this man born blind because he sinned? Or did his parents sin?"

"It isn't because this man sinned," said Jesus. "It isn't because his parents sinned. He was born blind so that God's power could be shown by what's going to happen. While it is still day, we must do the works of the one who sent me. Night is coming. Then no one can work. While I am in the world, I am the light of the world."

After he said this, he spit on the ground. He made some mud with the spit. Then he put the mud on the man's eyes. "Go," he told him. "Wash in the Pool of Siloam." So the man went and washed. And he came home able to see.

✺

Then came the Feast of Hanukkah at Jerusalem. It was winter. Jesus was in the temple courtyard walking in Solomon's Porch. The Jews who were gathered there around Jesus spoke to him. They said, "How long will you keep us waiting? If you are the Messiah, tell us plainly."

Jesus answered, "I did tell you. But you do not believe. The works that I do in my Father's name are a witness for me. But you do not believe, because you are not my sheep. My sheep listen to my voice. I know them, and they follow me. I give them eternal life, and they will never die. No one will steal them out of my hand. My Father, who has given them to me, is greater than anyone. No one can steal them out of my Father's hand. I and the Father are one."

Again the Jews who had challenged him picked up stones to kill him. Again they tried to arrest him. But he escaped from them. Then Jesus went back across the Jordan River.

⌒ჯჯ⌒

A man named Lazarus was sick. He was from Bethany, the village where Mary and her sister Martha lived. So the sisters sent a message to Jesus. "Lord," they told him, "the one you love is sick."

Jesus loved Martha and her sister and Lazarus. So after he heard Lazarus was sick, he stayed where he was for two more days. And then he said to his disciples, "Let us go back to Judea."

"But Rabbi," they said, "a short time ago the Jews there tried to kill you with stones. Are you still going back?"

Jesus answered, "Our friend Lazarus has fallen asleep. But I am going there to wake him up."

His disciples replied, "Lord, if he's sleeping, he will get better." Jesus had been speaking about the death of Lazarus. But his disciples thought he meant natural sleep.

So then he told them plainly, "Lazarus is dead. For your benefit, I am glad I was not there. Now you will believe. But let us go to him."

Then Thomas, who was also called Didymus, spoke to the rest of the disciples. "Let us go also," he said. "Then we can die with Jesus."

When Jesus arrived, he found out that Lazarus had already been in the tomb for four days. When Martha heard that Jesus was coming, she went out to meet him. But Mary stayed at home.

"Lord," Martha said to Jesus, "I wish you had been here! Then my brother would not have died. But I know that even now God will give you anything you ask for."

Jesus said to her, "Your brother will rise again."

Martha answered, "I know he will rise again. This will happen when people are raised from the dead on the last day."

Jesus said to her, "I am the resurrection and the life. Anyone who believes in me will live, even if they die. And whoever lives by believing in me will never die. Do you believe this?"

"Yes, Lord," she replied. "I believe that you are the Messiah, the Son of God. I believe that you are the one who is supposed to come into the world."

After she said this, she went back home. She called her sister Mary to one side to talk to her. "The Teacher is here," Martha said. "He is asking for you." When Mary heard this, she got up quickly and went to him. Some Jews had been comforting Mary in the house. They noticed how quickly she got up and went out. So they followed her. They thought she was going to the tomb to mourn there.

Mary reached the place where Jesus was. When she saw him, she fell at his feet. She said, "Lord, I wish you had been here! Then my brother would not have died."

Jesus saw her crying. He saw that the Jews who had come along with her were crying also. His spirit became very sad, and he was troubled. "Where have you put him?" he asked.

"Come and see, Lord," they replied.

Jesus wept.

Then the Jews said, "See how much he loved him!"

But some of them said, "He opened the eyes of the blind man. Couldn't he have kept this man from dying?"

Once more Jesus felt very sad. He came to the tomb. It was a cave with a stone in front of the entrance. "Take away the stone," he said.

"But, Lord," said Martha, the sister of the dead man, "by this time there is a bad smell. Lazarus has been in the tomb for four days."

Then Jesus said, "Didn't I tell you that if you believe, you will see God's glory?"

So they took away the stone. Then Jesus looked up. He said, "Father, I thank you for hearing me. I know that you always hear me. But I said this for the benefit of the people standing here. I said it so they will believe that you sent me."

Then Jesus called in a loud voice. He said, "Lazarus, come out!"

The dead man came out. His hands and feet were wrapped with strips of linen. A cloth was around his face.

Jesus said to them, "Take off the clothes he was buried in and let him go."

Many of the Jews who had come to visit Mary saw what Jesus did. So they believed in him. But some of them went to the Pharisees. They told the Pharisees what Jesus had done. Then the chief priests and the Pharisees called a meeting of the Sanhedrin.

"What can we do?" they asked. "This man is performing many signs. If we let him keep on doing this, everyone will believe in him. Then the Romans will come. They will take away our temple and our nation."

So from that day on, the Jewish rulers planned to kill Jesus.

Jesus no longer moved around openly among the people of Judea. Instead, he went away to an area near the desert.

It was almost time for the Jewish Passover Feast. Many people went up from the country to Jerusalem. They kept looking for Jesus as they stood in the temple courtyard. They asked one another, "What do you think? Isn't he coming to the feast at all?" But the chief priests and the Pharisees had given orders. They had commanded anyone who found out where Jesus was staying to report it. Then they could arrest him.

༺༼ঌ

It was six days before the Passover Feast. Jesus came to Bethany, where Lazarus lived. Lazarus was the one Jesus had raised from the dead. A dinner was given at Bethany to honor Jesus. Martha served the food. Lazarus was among the people at the table with Jesus. Then Mary took about a pint of pure nard. It was an expensive perfume. She poured it on Jesus' feet and wiped them with her hair. The house was filled with the sweet smell of the perfume.

But Judas Iscariot didn't like what Mary did. He was one of Jesus' disciples. Later he was going to hand Jesus over to his enemies. Judas said, "Why wasn't this perfume sold? Why wasn't the money given to poor people? It was worth a year's pay." He didn't say this because he cared about the poor. He said it because he was a thief.

Judas was in charge of the money bag. He used to help himself to what was in it.

"Leave her alone," Jesus replied. "The perfume was meant for the day I am buried. You will always have the poor among you. But you won't always have me."

♋

The next day the large crowd that had come for the feast heard that Jesus was on his way to Jerusalem. So they took branches from palm trees and went out to meet him. They shouted,

"Hosanna! "

"Blessed is the one who comes in the name of the Lord!"

"Blessed is the king of Israel!"

A crowd had been with Jesus when he called Lazarus from the tomb and raised him from the dead. So they continued to tell everyone about what had happened. Many people went out to meet him. They had heard that he had done this sign.

Jesus had performed so many signs in front of them. But they still would not believe in him.

At the same time that Jesus did those signs, many of the Jewish leaders believed in him. But because of the Pharisees, they would not openly admit they believed. They were afraid they would be thrown out of the synagogue. They loved praise from people more than praise from God.

remember what you read

1. What is something you noticed for the first time?

_____

_____

_____

_____

2. What questions did you have?

_____

_____

_____

_____

3. Was there anything that bothered you?

_____

_____

_____

_____

4. What did you learn about loving God?

_____

_____

_____

_____

5. What did you learn about loving others?

_____

_____

_____

_____

introduction to John, part 3

John wrote about Jesus because he wanted people to know that Jesus had been sent by God the Father. Everything Jesus did was planned by God.

In the final part of John's story, Jesus gets ready to go back to his Father. But the road won't be easy.

Before he leaves, Jesus promises to send his followers another "Friend" to watch over them. See if you can figure out who it is.

It was just before the Passover Feast. Jesus knew that the time had come for him to leave this world. It was time for him to go to the Father. Jesus loved his disciples who were in the world. So he now loved them to the very end.

They were having their evening meal. Jesus got up from the meal and took off his outer clothes. He wrapped a towel around his waist. After that, he poured water into a large bowl. Then he began to wash his disciples' feet.

"Do you understand what I have done for you?" he asked them. "You call me 'Teacher' and 'Lord.' You are right. That is what I am. I, your Lord and Teacher, have washed your feet. So you also should wash one another's feet. I have given you an example. You should do as I have done for you.

After he had said this, Jesus' spirit was troubled. He said, "What I'm about to tell you is true. One of you is going to hand me over to my enemies."

His disciples stared at one another. They had no idea which one of them he meant. The disciple Jesus loved was next to him at the table. He asked him, "Lord, who is it?"

Jesus answered, "It is the one I will give this piece of bread to. I will give it to him after I have dipped it in the dish." He dipped the piece of bread. Then he gave it to Judas, son of Simon Iscariot. As soon as Judas took the bread, Satan entered into him.

So Jesus told him, "Do quickly what you are going to do." As soon as Judas had taken the bread, he went out. And it was night.

After Judas was gone, Jesus spoke. He said, "My children, I will be with you only a little longer.

"I give you a new command. Love one another. You must love one another, just as I have loved you. If you love one another, everyone will know you are my disciples.

"Do not let your hearts be troubled. You believe in God. Believe in me also. There are many rooms in my Father's house. If this were not true, would I have told you that I am going there? Would I have told you that I would prepare a place for you there? If I go and do that, I will come back. And I will take you to be with me. Then you will also be where I am. You know the way to the place where I am going."

Thomas said to him, "Lord, we don't know where you are going. So how can we know the way?"

Jesus answered, "I am the way and the truth and the life. No one comes to the Father except through me. If you really know me, you will know my Father also. From now on, you do know him. And you have seen him.

"I will ask the Father. And he will give you another friend to help you and to be with you forever. The Friend is the Holy Spirit. He will teach you all things. He will remind you of everything I have said to you. I leave my peace with you. Do not let your hearts be troubled.

"Come now. Let us leave.

They crossed the Kidron Valley. On the other side there was a garden. Jesus and his disciples went into it.

Judas knew the place. Jesus had often met in that place with his disciples. So Judas came to the garden. He was guiding a group of soldiers and some officials. The chief priests and the Pharisees had sent them. They were carrying torches, lanterns and weapons. Jesus knew everything that was going to happen to him. So he went out and asked them, "Who do you want?"

"Jesus of Nazareth," they replied.

"I am he," Jesus said. Then they fell to the ground.

He asked them again, "Who do you want?"

"Jesus of Nazareth," they said.

Jesus answered, "I told you I am he. If you are looking for me, then let these men go."

Simon Peter had a sword and pulled it out. He struck the high priest's slave and cut off his right ear. The slave's name was Malchus.

Jesus commanded Peter, "Put your sword away! Shouldn't I drink the cup of suffering the Father has given me?"

Then the group of soldiers, their commander and the Jewish officials arrested Jesus. They tied him up and brought him first to Annas. He was the father-in-law of Caiaphas, the high priest at that time.

ᘉᘉᘉ

Then the Jewish leaders took Jesus from Caiaphas to the palace of the Roman governor. Pilate came out to them. He asked, "What charges are you bringing against this man?"

"He has committed crimes," they replied. "If he hadn't, we would not have handed him over to you."

Then Pilate went back inside the palace. He ordered Jesus to be brought to him. Pilate asked him, "Are you the king of the Jews?"

"Is that your own idea?" Jesus asked. "Or did others talk to you about me?"

"Am I a Jew?" Pilate replied. "Your own people and chief priests handed you over to me. What have you done?"

Jesus said, "My kingdom is not from this world. If it were, those who serve me would fight. My kingdom is from another place."

"So you are a king, then!" said Pilate.

Jesus answered, "You say that I am a king. Everyone who is on the side of truth listens to me."

"What is truth?" Pilate replied.

Then Pilate took Jesus and had him whipped. The soldiers twisted thorns together to make a crown. They put it on Jesus' head. Then they put a purple robe on him.

Once more Pilate came out. He said to the Jews gathered there, "Look, I am bringing Jesus out to you. I want to let you know that I find no basis for a charge against him." Jesus came out wearing the crown of thorns and the purple robe.

As soon as the chief priests and their officials saw him, they shouted, "Crucify him! Crucify him!"

But Pilate answered, "You take him and crucify him. I myself find no basis for a charge against him."

The Jewish leaders replied, "We have a law. That law says he must die. He claimed to be the Son of God."

When Pilate heard that, he was even more afraid. He went back inside the palace. "Where do you come from?" he asked Jesus. But Jesus did not answer him. "Do you refuse to speak to me?" Pilate said. "Don't you understand? I have the power to set you free or to nail you to a cross."

Jesus answered, "You were given power from heaven. If you weren't, you would have no power over me. So the one who handed me over to you is guilty of a greater sin."

From then on, Pilate tried to set Jesus free. But the Jewish leaders kept shouting, "If you let this man go, you are not Caesar's friend! Anyone who claims to be a king is against Caesar!"

Finally, Pilate handed Jesus over to them to be nailed to a cross.

So the soldiers took charge of Jesus. He had to carry his own cross. He went out to a place called the Skull. There they nailed Jesus to the cross.

Pilate had a notice prepared. It was fastened to the cross. It read,

JESUS OF NAZARETH, THE KING OF THE JEWS.

Later, Jesus said, "I am thirsty." A jar of wine vinegar was there. So they soaked a sponge in it. They put the sponge on the stem of a hyssop plant. Then they lifted it up to Jesus' lips. After Jesus drank he said, "It is finished." Then he bowed his head and died.

ᏅᎦᎣ

Later Joseph asked Pilate for Jesus' body. Joseph was from the town of Arimathea. He was a follower of Jesus. But he followed Jesus secretly because he was afraid of the Jewish leaders. After Pilate gave him permission, Joseph came and took the body away. Nicodemus went with Joseph. He was the man who had earlier visited Jesus at night. Nicodemus brought some mixed spices that weighed about 75 pounds. The two men took Jesus' body. They wrapped it in strips of linen cloth, along with the spices. That was the way the Jews buried people. At the place where Jesus was crucified, there was a garden. A new tomb was there. No one had ever been put in it before. So they placed Jesus there.

Early on the first day of the week, Mary Magdalene went to the tomb. It was still dark. She saw that the stone had been moved away from the entrance. So she ran to Simon Peter and another disciple, the one Jesus loved. She said, "They have taken the Lord out of the tomb! We don't know where they have put him!"

So Peter and the other disciple started out for the tomb. Both of them were running. The other disciple ran faster than Peter. He reached the tomb first. He bent over and looked in at the strips of linen lying there. But he did not go in. Then Simon Peter came along behind him. He went straight into the tomb. He saw the strips of linen lying there. He also saw the funeral cloth that had been wrapped around Jesus' head. The disciple who had reached the tomb first also went inside. He saw and believed. They still did not understand from Scripture that Jesus had to rise from the dead. Then the disciples went back to where they were staying.

But Mary stood outside the tomb crying. As she cried, she bent over to look into the tomb. She saw two angels dressed in white. They were seated where Jesus' body had been. One of them was where Jesus' head had been laid. The other sat where his feet had been placed.

They asked her, "Woman, why are you crying?"

"They have taken my Lord away," she said. "I don't know where they have put him." Then she turned around and saw Jesus standing there. But she didn't realize that it was Jesus.

He asked her, "Woman, why are you crying? Who are you looking for?"

She thought he was the gardener. So she said, "Sir, did you carry him away? Tell me where you put him. Then I will go and get him."

Jesus said to her, "Mary."

She turned toward him. Then she cried out in the Aramaic language, *"Rabboni!"* Rabboni means Teacher.

Jesus said, "Do not hold on to me. I have not yet ascended to the Father. Instead, go to those who believe in me. Tell them, 'I am ascending to my Father and your Father, to my God and your God.'"

Mary Magdalene went to the disciples with the news. She said, "I have seen the Lord!"

On the evening of that first day of the week, the disciples were together. They had locked the doors because they were afraid of the Jewish leaders. Jesus came in and stood among them. He said, "May peace be with you!" Then he showed them his hands and his side. The disciples were very happy when they saw the Lord.

Again Jesus said, "May peace be with you! The Father has sent me. So now I am sending you." He then breathed on them. He said, "Receive the Holy Spirit. If you forgive anyone's sins, their sins are forgiven. If you do not forgive them, they are not forgiven."

Jesus performed many other signs in front of his disciples. They are not written down in this book. But these are written so that you may believe that Jesus is the Messiah, the Son of God. If you believe this, you will have life because you belong to him.

remember what you read

1. What is something you noticed for the first time?

_____

_____

_____

_____

2. What questions did you have?

_____

_____

_____

_____

3. Was there anything that bothered you?

_____

_____

_____

_____

4. What did you learn about loving God?

_____

_____

_____

_____

5. What did you learn about loving others?

_____

_____

_____

_____

introduction to 1 John

In today's reading, we have three letters from John, the disciple of Jesus.

Several years after Jesus rose from the dead, trouble was brewing for one church. Many of its members had left because they couldn't stomach the idea that Jesus, the Son of God, had come to earth in a human body.

Why did they have such a hard time with this?

Well, because back then, it was popular to believe that everything physical was bad. God couldn't possibly show up in a human body! Only spiritual things which couldn't be seen or touched were any good.

Or so that's how the thinking went.

As a result, some people—even within the church—began denying that Jesus had really come in the flesh. Not only this, but they were treating others badly. They were refusing to love one another. They claimed they knew better than everyone else, and so they walked out.

Those who were left behind were badly shaken, hurt, and confused.

John, the same one who wrote our last story about Jesus, sent a letter to encourage those who had stayed faithful to Jesus. He assured them that Jesus really had come in the flesh. After all, John had seen Jesus with his own eyes. He reminded them that one unmistakable sign of a real Jesus follower is love. If we don't love one another, he said, then we don't love God.

As you read John's letter, think about who you can show God's love to today.

Here is what we announce to everyone about the Word of life. The Word was already here from the beginning. We have heard him. We have seen him with our eyes. We have looked at him. Our hands have touched him.

We announce to you what we have seen and heard. We do it so you can share life together with us. And we share life with the Father and with his Son, Jesus Christ. We are writing this to make our joy complete.

Here is the message we have heard from him and announce to you. God is light. There is no darkness in him at all. Suppose we say that we share life with God but still walk in the darkness. Then we are lying. We are not living out the truth. But suppose we walk in the light, just as he is in the light. Then we share life with one another. And the blood of Jesus, his Son, makes us pure from all sin.

Suppose we claim we are without sin. Then we are fooling ourselves. The truth is not in us. But God is faithful and fair. If we confess our sins, he will forgive our sins. He will forgive every wrong thing we have done. He will make us pure.

My dear children, I'm writing this to you so that you will not sin. But suppose someone does sin. Then we have a friend who speaks to the Father for us. He is Jesus Christ, the Blameless One. He gave his life to pay for our sins. But he not only paid for our sins. He also paid for the sins of the whole world.

We know that we have come to know God if we obey his commands. Suppose someone says, "I know him." But suppose this person does not do what God commands. Then this person is a liar and is not telling the truth. But if anyone obeys God's word, then that person truly loves God. Here is how we know we belong to him. Those who claim to belong to him must live just as Jesus did.

We know what love is because Jesus Christ gave his life for us. So we should give our lives for our brothers and sisters. Suppose someone sees a brother or sister in need and is able to help them. And suppose that person doesn't take pity on these needy people. Then how can the love of God be in that person? Dear children, don't just talk about love. Put your love into action. Then it will truly be love.

God has commanded us to believe in the name of his Son, Jesus Christ. He has also commanded us to love one another. The one who obeys God's commands remains joined to him. And he remains joined to them. Here is how we know that God lives in us. We know it because of the Holy Spirit he gave us.

Dear friends, do not believe every spirit. Test the spirits to see if they belong to God. Many false prophets have gone out into the world. Here is how you can recognize the Spirit of God. Every spirit agreeing that Jesus Christ came in a human body belongs to God. But every spirit that doesn't agree with this does not belong to God.

Dear children, you belong to God. You have not accepted the teachings of the false prophets. That's because the one who is in you is powerful. He is more powerful than the one who is in the world.

Dear friends, let us love one another, because love comes from God. Everyone who loves has become a child of God and knows God. Anyone who does not love does not know God, because God is love. Here is how God showed his love among us. He sent his one and only Son into the world. He sent him so we could receive life through him. Here is what love is. It is not that we loved God. It is that he loved us and sent his Son to give his life to pay for our sins. Dear friends, since God loved us this much, we should also love one another.

The Father has sent his Son to be the Savior of the world. We have seen it and are witnesses to it. God lives in anyone who agrees that Jesus is the Son of God. This kind of person remains joined to God. So we know that God loves us. We depend on it.

God is love. Anyone who leads a life of love is joined to God. And God is joined to them. Suppose love is fulfilled among us. Then we can be without fear on the day God judges the world. Love is fulfilled among us when in this world we are like Jesus. There is no fear in love. Instead, perfect love drives away fear. That's because fear has to do with being punished. The one who fears does not have perfect love.

We love because he loved us first. Suppose someone claims to love God but hates a brother or sister. Then they are a liar. They don't love their brother or sister, whom they have seen. So they can't love God, whom they haven't seen. Here is the command God has given us. Anyone who loves God must also love their brother and sister.

I'm writing these things to you who believe in the name of the Son of God. I'm writing so you will know that you have eternal life.

introduction to 2 John

So that was John's first letter, but it wasn't his only letter. There were other groups of Jesus-followers who weren't sure what to believe. So John wrote a second letter to a church he called "the chosen lady." He wanted to encourage them to keep on loving each other—and to warn them about false teachers who were spreading lies about Jesus. But John kept this letter short, because was hoping to encourage these believers face to face.

ᴄᴏᴏ

I, the elder, am writing this letter.

I am sending it to the lady chosen by God and to her children. I love all of you because of the truth. I love you because of the truth that is alive in us. This truth will be with us forever.

God the Father and Jesus Christ his Son will give you grace, mercy and peace. These blessings will be with us because we love the truth.

It has given me great joy to find some of your children living by the truth. That's just what the Father commanded us to do. Dear lady, I'm not writing you a new command. I'm writing a command we've had from the beginning. I'm asking that we love one another. The way we show our love is to obey God's commands. He commands you to lead a life of love. That's what you have heard from the beginning.

I say this because many people have tried to fool others. These people have gone out into the world. They don't agree that Jesus

Christ came in a human body. People like this try to trick others. These people are like the great enemy of Christ. Watch out that you don't lose what we have worked for. Make sure that you get your full reward.

I have a lot to write to you. But I don't want to use paper and ink. I hope I can visit you instead. Then I can talk with you face to face. That will make our joy complete.

The children of your sister, who is chosen by God, send their greetings.

introduction to 3 John

John's third letter was written to a friend named Gaius, who had opened his doors to a group of believers who were traveling around, preaching the truth about Jesus.
Gaius had shown them kindness at great personal risk, because a renegade leader named Diotrephes didn't want anyone to help the traveling believers. John wrote to thank Gaius and encourage him to keep on doing what was right.

I, the elder, am writing this letter.

I am sending it to you, my dear friend Gaius. I love you because of the truth.

Some believers came to me and told me that you are faithful to the truth. They told me that you continue to live by it. This news gave me great joy.

Dear friend, you are faithful in what you are doing for the brothers and sisters. You are faithful even though they are strangers to you. They have told the church about your love. They started on their journey to serve Jesus Christ. They didn't receive any help from those who aren't believers. So we should welcome people like them. We should work together with them for the truth.

I wrote to the church. But Diotrephes will not welcome us. He loves to be the first in everything. So when I come, I will point out what he is doing. He is saying evil things that aren't true about us. Even this doesn't satisfy him. So he refuses to welcome other believers. He also keeps others from welcoming them. In fact, he throws them out of the church.

Dear friend, don't be like those who do evil. Be like those who do good. Anyone who does what is good belongs to God. Anyone who does what is evil hasn't really seen or known God.

I have a lot to write to you. But I don't want to write with pen and ink. I hope I can see you soon. Then we can talk face to face.

May you have peace.

The friends here send their greetings. Greet each one of the friends there.

remember what you read

1. What is something you noticed for the first time?

_____

_____

_____

_____

2. What questions did you have?

_____

_____

_____

_____

3. Was there anything that bothered you?

_____

_____

_____

_____

4. What did you learn about loving God?

_____

_____

_____

_____

5. What did you learn about loving others?

_____

_____

_____

_____

introduction to Revelation, part 1

*We've had quite a journey through the New Testament so far.
We've heard four different writers tell the amazing story of Jesus.
We've listened in on letters that were sent to some of the very first
Christians. Now it's time for one last story: this one from the book of
Revelation.*

*In the early days of the church, the Roman Empire was the most
powerful kingdom on earth. Over time, the kings of Rome, known as
Caesars, grew very proud. They began to think of themselves as gods.
They demanded to be worshiped and revered.*

*This put followers of Jesus in a dangerous position. They believed
there was only one God—that Jesus is Lord, not Caesar. But if they
didn't bow down to Caesar, they could lose everything. They could
even be put to death.*

*In the midst of all this, a prophet named John had a vision. He
shared it with seven churches located in a realm of the empire known
as Asia Minor.*

*In the first part of John's vision, Jesus speaks directly to the seven
churches. He encourages those who have stayed faithful to him, telling
them to hang in there, even if it means laying down their lives. And he
warns those who haven't been faithful to turn around before it's too
late.*

*In spite of the dangers they face, there is good news for followers of
Jesus. According to Revelation, those who "overcome" will live forever.*

*This is the revelation from Jesus Christ. God gave it to him to
show those who serve God what will happen soon. God made it
known by sending his angel to his servant John. John is a witness to*

everything he saw. What he saw is God's word and what Jesus Christ has said. Blessed is the one who reads out loud the words of this prophecy. Blessed are those who hear it and think everything it says is important. The time when these things will come true is near.

⟶⟶⟶

I, John, am writing this letter.

May grace and peace come to you from God. He is the one who is, and who was, and who will come. May grace and peace come to you from Jesus Christ. He is the faithful witness, so what he has shown can be trusted. He was the first to rise from the dead. He rules over the kings of the earth.

Glory and power belong to Jesus Christ for ever and ever! Amen.

"Look! He is coming with the clouds!"
"Every eye will see him.
Even those who pierced him will see him."
All the nations of the earth "will mourn because of him."
This will really happen! Amen.

"I am the Alpha and the Omega, the Beginning and the End," says the Lord God. "I am the God who is, and who was, and who will come. I am the Mighty One."

⟶⟶⟶

I, John, am a believer like you. I am a friend who suffers like you. I was on the island of Patmos because I taught God's word and what Jesus said. The Holy Spirit gave me a vision on the Lord's Day. I heard a loud voice behind me that sounded like a trumpet. The voice said, "Write on a scroll what you see."

I turned around to see who was speaking to me. When I turned, I saw seven golden lampstands. In the middle of them was someone who looked "like a son of man." He was dressed in a long robe with a gold strip of cloth around his chest. The hair on his head was white like wool, as white as snow. His eyes were like a blazing fire. His feet were like bronze metal glowing in a furnace. His voice sounded like rushing waters. He held seven stars in his right hand. Coming out of his mouth was a sharp sword with two edges. His face was like the sun shining in all its brightness.

When I saw him, I fell at his feet as if I were dead. Then he put his right hand on me and said, "Do not be afraid. I am the First and the Last. I am the Living One. I was dead. But now look! I am alive for ever and ever!

"So write down what you have seen. Write about what is happening now and what will happen later. Here is the meaning of the mystery of the seven stars you saw in my right hand. They are the angels of the seven churches. And the seven golden lampstands you saw stand for the seven churches.

෨ᘔᘔᕦ

"Here is what I command you to write to the church in Ephesus.

'I know what you are doing. You work long and hard. You have been faithful and have put up with a lot of trouble because of me.

'But here is something I hold against you. You have turned away from the love you had at first. Think about how far you have fallen! Turn away from your sins. Do the things you did at first. If you don't, I will come to you and remove your lampstand from its place.

'Whoever has ears should listen to what the Holy Spirit says to the churches.' "

෨ᘔᘔᕦ

"Here is what I command you to write to the church in Smyrna.

'I know that you suffer and are poor. But you are rich! Don't be afraid of what you are going to suffer. I tell you, the devil will put some of you in prison to test you. Be faithful, even if it means you must die. Then I will give you life as your crown of victory.

'Whoever has ears should listen to what the Holy Spirit says to the churches. Here is what I will do for anyone who has victory over sin. I will not let that person be hurt at all by the second death.' "

⚬♋⚬

"Here is what I command you to write to the church in Pergamum.

'I know that you live where Satan has his throne. But you remain faithful to me. You did not give up your faith in me.

'But I have a few things against you. Some of your people follow the teaching of Balaam. He taught Balak to lead the people of Israel into sin. So they ate food that had been offered to statues of gods. You also have people who follow the teaching of the Nicolaitans. So turn away from your sins! If you don't, I will come to you soon.

'Whoever has ears should listen to what the Holy Spirit says to the churches.' "

⚬♋⚬

"Here is what I command you to write to the church in Thyatira.

'I know your love and your faith. I know how well you have served.

'But here is what I have against you. You put up with that woman Jezebel. She calls herself a prophet. I've given her time to turn away from her sinful ways. But she doesn't want to. Those who commit adultery with her will suffer greatly too. Their only way out is to turn away from what she taught them to do.

'I won't ask the rest of you in Thyatira to do anything else. You don't follow the teaching of Jezebel. Just hold on to what you have until I come.

'Whoever has ears should listen to what the Holy Spirit says to the churches.' "

⚬♋⚬

"Here is what I command you to write to the church in Sardis.

'I know what you are doing. People think you are alive, but you are dead. Wake up! So remember what you have been taught and have heard. Hold firmly to it. Turn away from your sins. If you don't wake up, I will come like a thief.

'But you have a few people in Sardis who are pure. They will walk with me, dressed in white, because they are worthy. I will never erase their names from the book of life. Whoever has ears should listen to what the Holy Spirit says to the churches.' "

∽∬∾

"Here is what I command you to write to the church in Philadelphia.

'I know that you don't have much strength. But you have obeyed my word. You have kept my command to remain strong in the faith no matter what happens. So I will keep you from the time of suffering. That time is going to come to the whole world.

'I am coming soon. Hold on to what you have. Then no one will take away your crown. Whoever has ears should listen to what the Holy Spirit says to the churches.' "

∽∬∾

"Here is what I command you to write to the church in Laodicea.

'I know what you are doing. I know you aren't cold or hot. I wish you were either one or the other! But you are lukewarm. You aren't hot or cold. So I am going to spit you out of my mouth. You say, "I am rich. I've become wealthy and don't need anything." But you don't realize how pitiful and miserable you have become. You are poor, blind and naked. So here's my advice. Buy from me gold made pure by fire. Then you will become rich. Buy from me white clothes to wear. Then you will be able to cover the shame of your naked bodies. And buy from me healing lotion to put on your eyes. Then you will be able to see.

'I warn and correct those I love. So be sincere, and turn away from your sins. Here I am! I stand at the door and knock. If anyone hears my voice and opens the door, I will come in. I will eat with that person, and they will eat with me.

'Here is what I will do for anyone who has victory over sin. I will give that person the right to sit with me on my throne. Whoever has ears should listen to what the Holy Spirit says to the churches.'"

remember what you read

1. What is something you noticed for the first time?

_____

_____

_____

_____

2. What questions did you have?

_____

_____

_____

_____

3. Was there anything that bothered you?

_____

_____

_____

_____

4. What did you learn about loving God?

_____

_____

_____

_____

5. What did you learn about loving others?

_____

_____

_____

_____

introduction to Revelation, part 2

The early followers of Jesus had a difficult choice to make: worship the Roman emperor or pay the price. Those who refused to bow down were persecuted. Many were killed. With no end in sight, followers of Jesus started wondering if God would ever come through for them.

So God send a vision to a prophet named John. In the first part of his vision, John shared specific words of warning and encouragement with seven churches.

In the next part, John talks about how he was taken up to heaven— to the very throne room of God! There, John watches a wild display as God brings judgment against his enemies and protects those who belong to him.

John uses a lot of strange images to describe what's happening. Many of them are hard to understand. But through it all, the message is this: Jesus will win in the end. Until then, he wants us to hang in there and stay true to him, no matter what the cost.

 ❧

After this I looked, and there in front of me was a door standing open in heaven. I heard the voice I had heard before. It sounded like a trumpet. The voice said, "Come up here. I will show you what must happen after this." At once the Holy Spirit gave me a vision. There in front of me was a throne in heaven with someone sitting on it.

Twenty-four other thrones surrounded that throne. Twenty-four elders were sitting on them. The elders were dressed in white. They had gold crowns on their heads.

In the inner circle, around the throne, were four living creatures. They were covered with eyes, in front and in back. Day and night, they never stop saying,

> "Holy, holy, holy
> is the Lord God who rules over all."

Then I saw a scroll in the right hand of the one sitting on the throne. The scroll had writing on both sides. It was sealed with seven seals. I saw a mighty angel calling out in a loud voice. He said, "Who is worthy to break the seals and open the scroll?" I cried and cried. That's because no one was found who was worthy to open the scroll or look inside. Then one of the elders said to me, "Do not cry! The Lion of the tribe of Judah has won the battle. He is able to break the seven seals and open the scroll."

Then I saw a Lamb that looked as if he had been put to death. The Lamb went and took the scroll. He took it from the right hand of the one sitting on the throne. Then the four living creatures and the 24 elders fell down in front of the Lamb. Here is the new song they sang.

> "You are worthy to take the scroll
>   and break open its seals.
> You are worthy because you were put to death.
>   With your blood you bought people for God.
>   They come from every tribe, people and nation,
>   no matter what language they speak.
> You have made them members of a royal family.
>   You have made them priests to serve our God.
>   They will rule on the earth."

Then I looked and heard the voice of millions and millions of angels. They surrounded the throne. They surrounded the living creatures and the elders. In a loud voice they were saying,

> "The Lamb, who was put to death, is worthy!
>   He is worthy to receive power and wealth and wisdom and
>   strength!
>   He is worthy to receive honor and glory and praise!"

All creatures in heaven, on earth, under the earth, and on the sea were speaking. The whole creation was speaking.

⟳

I watched as the Lamb broke open the first of the seven seals. There in front of me was a white horse! Its rider held a bow in his hands. He was given a crown. He rode out like a hero on his way to victory.

The Lamb broke open the second seal. Another horse came out. It was red like fire. Its rider was given power to take peace from the earth. He was given power to make people kill each other.

The Lamb broke open the third seal. I looked, and there in front of me was a black horse! Its rider was holding a pair of scales in his hand. Next, I heard what sounded like a voice coming from among the four living creatures. It said, "Two pounds of wheat for a day's pay. And six pounds of barley for a day's pay. And leave the olive oil and the wine alone!"

The Lamb broke open the fourth seal. I looked, and there in front of me was a pale horse! Its rider's name was Death. Following close behind him was Hell. They were given power to kill people by swords. They could also use hunger, sickness and the earth's wild animals to kill.

The Lamb broke open the fifth seal. I saw souls under the altar. They were the souls of people who had been killed. They had been killed because of God's word and their faithful witness. They called out in a loud voice. "How long, Lord and King, holy and true?" they asked. "How long will you wait to judge those who live on the earth? How long will it be until you pay them back for killing us?" Then each of them was given a white robe. "Wait a little longer," they were told.

I watched as the Lamb broke open the sixth seal. There was a powerful earthquake. The stars in the sky fell to earth.

Everyone hid in caves and among the rocks of the mountains. They called out to the mountains and rocks, "Fall on us! Hide us from the anger of the Lamb!"

⟳

After this I saw four angels. They were standing at the four corners of the earth. Then I saw another angel coming up from the east. He brought the official seal of the living God. Then I heard how many people were marked with the seal. There were 144,000 from all the tribes of Israel.

After this I looked, and there in front of me was a huge crowd of people. They stood in front of the throne and in front of the Lamb. There were so many that no one could count them. They came from every nation, tribe and people. That's true no matter what language they spoke. They were wearing white robes. In their hands they were holding palm branches. They cried out in a loud voice,

"Salvation belongs to our God,
who sits on the throne.
Salvation also belongs to the Lamb."

Then one of the elders spoke to me. "Who are these people dressed in white robes?"

I answered, "Sir, you know."

He said, "They are the ones who have come out of the time of terrible suffering. They have washed their robes and made them white in the blood of the Lamb.

'He will lead them to springs of living water.'
'And God will wipe away every tear from their eyes.'"

The Lamb opened the seventh seal. Then there was silence in heaven for about half an hour.

⌁

I saw the seven angels who stand in front of God. Seven trumpets were given to them.

The first angel blew his trumpet. Hail and fire mixed with blood were thrown down on the earth. A third of the earth was burned up. A third of the trees were burned up. All the green grass was burned up.

The second angel blew his trumpet. Something that looked like a huge mountain on fire was thrown into the sea.

The third angel blew his trumpet. Then a great star fell from the sky.

The fourth angel blew his trumpet. Then a third of the sun was struck. A third of the moon was struck. A third of the stars were struck.

The fifth angel blew his trumpet. Then I saw a star that had fallen from the sky to the earth. The star was given the key to the tunnel leading down into a bottomless pit. The pit was called the Abyss. The star opened the Abyss. Then smoke rose up from it like the smoke from a huge furnace. Out of the smoke came locusts. They came down on the earth. They were told not to harm the grass of the earth or any plant or tree. They were supposed to harm only the people without God's official seal on their foreheads. In those days, people will look for a way to die but won't find it. They will want to die, but death will escape them.

The sixth angel blew his trumpet. Then I heard a voice coming from the four corners of the golden altar. The altar stands in front of God. The voice said, "Set the four angels free who are held at the great river Euphrates." The four angels had been ready for this very hour and day and month and year. They were set free to kill a third of all people.

There were people who were not killed by these plagues. But they still didn't turn away from what they had been doing. They kept worshiping statues of gods made out of gold, silver, bronze, stone and wood. These statues can't see or hear or walk.

The seventh angel blew his trumpet. There were loud voices in heaven. They said,

"The kingdom of the world has become
   the kingdom of our Lord and of his Messiah.
He will rule for ever and ever."

◌ჯჯი

A great sign appeared in heaven. It was a woman wearing the sun like clothes. The moon was under her feet. On her head she wore a crown of 12 stars. She was pregnant. She cried out in pain because she was about to have a baby. Then another sign appeared in heaven. It was a huge red dragon. The dragon stood in front of the woman who was about to have a baby. The dragon wanted to eat her child the moment he was born. She gave birth to a son. He "will rule all the nations with an iron scepter." And her child was taken up to God and to his throne.

The woman was given the two wings of a great eagle. She was given these wings so that she could fly away. She could fly to the place prepared for her in the desert. There she would be taken care of for three and a half years. The dragon was very angry with the woman. He went off to make war against the rest of her children. They obey God's commands. And they hold firmly to the truth they have said about Jesus.

The dragon stood on the seashore. I saw a beast coming out of the sea. It had ten horns and seven heads. The dragon gave the beast his power, his throne, and great authority. One of the beast's heads seemed to have had a deadly wound. But the wound had been healed. The whole world was amazed and followed the beast.

Then I saw a second beast. This one came out of the earth. It made the earth and all who live on it worship the first beast. The second beast ordered people to set up a statue to honor the first beast. The statue could kill all who refused to worship it. It also forced everyone to receive a mark on their right hand or on their forehead. They could not buy or sell anything unless they had the mark. The mark is the name of the beast.

∽◊◊◊∾

I looked, and there in front of me was the Lamb. He was standing on Mount Zion. With him were 144,000 people. Written on their foreheads were his name and his Father's name.

God's people need to be very patient. They are the ones who obey God's commands. And they remain faithful to Jesus.

Then I heard a voice from heaven. "Write this," it said. "Blessed are the dead who die as believers in the Lord from now on."

"Yes," says the Holy Spirit. "They will rest from their labor. What they have done will not be forgotten."

∽ᴔᴔᴕ

I saw in heaven another great and wonderful sign. Seven angels were about to bring the seven last plagues. The plagues would complete God's anger.

After this I looked, and I saw the temple in heaven. And it was opened. Then one of the four living creatures gave seven golden bowls to the seven angels. The bowls were filled with the anger of God, who lives for ever and ever.

Then I heard a loud voice from the temple speaking to the seven angels. "Go," it said. "Pour out the seven bowls of God's great anger on the earth."

remember what you read

1. What is something you noticed for the first time?

_____

_____

_____

_____

2. What questions did you have?

_____

_____

_____

_____

3. Was there anything that bothered you?

_____

_____

_____

_____

4. What did you learn about loving God?

_____

_____

_____

_____

5. What did you learn about loving others?

_____

_____

_____

_____

introduction to Revelation, part 3

Long ago, a prophet named John had a vision. He was taken up to heaven, where he saw how God will get rid of evil and rescue those who love him.

In our last reading, John watched as seven angels took seven bowls filled with God's anger and poured them out on the earth, punishing those who hurt God's people and cursed his name.

Today, John has a front-row seat for the final battle between God and his enemies. And he gets a sneak peak at a brand new earth waiting for those who follow God till the end.

John's Revelation is the last book in the New Testament. But it's not the end of the story, because each of us has a part to play. God want us to join him in making a new world by sharing the good news about Jesus and spreading hope and peace wherever we go.

And in the end, God himself will come back. He will make his home with us forever, and he'll make everything right.

I saw heaven standing open. There in front of me was a white horse. Its rider is called Faithful and True. His eyes are like blazing fire. On his head are many crowns. A name is written on him that only he knows. The armies of heaven were following him, riding on white horses. They were dressed in fine linen, white and clean. Coming out of the rider's mouth is a sharp sword. Here is the name that is written on the rider's robe and on his thigh.

THE GREATEST KING OF ALL AND THE
MOST POWERFUL LORD OF ALL

Then I saw the beast and the kings of the earth with their armies. They had gathered together to make war against the rider on the horse and his army. But the beast and the false prophet were captured. The false prophet had done signs for the beast. In this way the false prophet had tricked some people. Those people had received the mark of the beast and had worshiped its statue. The beast and the false prophet were thrown alive into the lake of fire. The lake of fire burns with sulfur. The rest were killed by the sword that came out of the rider's mouth.

⚬⟊⟊⟋

I saw an angel coming down out of heaven. He grabbed the dragon, that old serpent. The serpent is also called the devil, or Satan. The angel put him in chains for 1,000 years. Then he threw him into the Abyss.

I saw thrones. Those who had been given authority to judge were sitting on them. I also saw the souls of those whose heads had been cut off. They had been killed because they had spoken what was true about Jesus. They had also been killed because of the word of God. They had not worshiped the beast or its statue. They had not received its mark on their foreheads or hands. They came to life and ruled with Christ for 1,000 years.

When the 1,000 years are over, Satan will be set free from his prison. He will go out to cause the nations to believe lies. He will gather them from the four corners of the earth. Their troops are as many as the grains of sand on the seashore. They marched across the whole earth. They surrounded the place where God's holy people were camped. But fire came down from heaven and burned them up. The devil had caused them to believe lies. He was thrown into the lake of burning sulfur. That is where the beast and the false prophet had been thrown. They will all suffer day and night for ever and ever.

⚬⟊⟊⟋

I saw a great white throne. And I saw God sitting on it. I saw the dead, great and small, standing in front of the throne. Books were opened. Then another book was opened. It was the book of life. The dead were judged by what they had done. The things they had done were written in the books. Then Death and Hell were thrown into the lake of fire. The lake of fire is the second death. Anyone whose name was not written in the book of life was thrown into the lake of fire.

⚬ᘓᘓᘔ⚬

I saw "a new heaven and a new earth." The first heaven and the first earth were completely gone. I heard a loud voice from the throne. It said, "Look! God now makes his home with the people. He will live with them. They will be his people. And God himself will be with them and be their God. 'He will wipe away every tear from their eyes. There will be no more death.' And there will be no more sadness. There will be no more crying or pain. Things are no longer the way they used to be."

He who was sitting on the throne said, "I am making everything new!"

He said to me, "It is done. I am the Alpha and the Omega, the Beginning and the End. I will give water to anyone who is thirsty. The water will come from the spring of the water of life. It doesn't cost anything! Those who have victory will receive all this from me. I will be their God, and they will be my children.

⚬ᘓᘓᘔ⚬

One of the seven angels who had the seven bowls came and spoke to me. The angel said, "Come. I will show you the bride, the wife of the Lamb." Then he carried me away in a vision. The Spirit took me to a huge, high mountain. He showed me Jerusalem, the Holy City. It was coming down out of heaven from God. It shone with the glory of God.

The city had a huge, high wall with 12 gates. On the gates were written the names of the 12 tribes of Israel.

The wall of the city had 12 foundations. Written on them were the names of the 12 apostles of the Lamb.

The city was laid out like a square. It was 1,400 miles long. It was as wide and high as it was long.

The wall was made out of jasper. The city was made out of pure gold, as pure as glass. The foundations of the city walls were decorated with every kind of jewel.

I didn't see a temple in the city. That's because the Lamb and the Lord God who rules over all are its temple. The city does not need the sun or moon to shine on it. God's glory is its light, and the Lamb is its lamp.

The nations will walk by the light of the city. The kings of the world will bring their glory into it. Its gates will never be shut, because there will be no night there. The glory and honor of the nations will be brought into it. Only what is pure will enter the city. Only those whose names are written in the Lamb's book of life will enter the city.

Then the angel showed me the river of the water of life. It was as clear as crystal. It flowed from the throne of God and of the Lamb. It flowed down the middle of the city's main street. On each side of the river stood the tree of life, bearing 12 crops of fruit. Its fruit was ripe every month. The leaves of the tree bring healing to the nations. There will no longer be any curse.

The throne of God and of the Lamb will be in the city. God's servants will serve him. They will see his face. His name will be on their foreheads. There will be no more night. They will not need the light of a lamp or the light of the sun. The Lord God will give them light. They will rule for ever and ever.

The angel said to me, "You can trust these words. They are true. The Lord is the God who gives messages to the prophets. He sent his angel to show his servants the things that must soon take place."

"Look! I am coming soon! I will reward each person for what they have done. I am the Alpha and the Omega. I am the First and the Last. I am the Beginning and the End.

"Blessed are those who wash their robes. They will have the

right to come to the tree of life. They will be allowed to go through the gates into the city.

"I, Jesus, have sent my angel to give you this witness for the churches. I am the Root and the Son of David. I am the bright Morning Star."

The Holy Spirit and the bride say, "Come!" And the person who hears should say, "Come!" Anyone who is thirsty should come. Anyone who wants to take the free gift of the water of life should do so.

Jesus is a witness about these things. He says, "Yes. I am coming soon."

Amen. Come, Lord Jesus!

remember what you read

1. What is something you noticed for the first time?

_____

_____

_____

_____

2. What questions did you have?

_____

_____

_____

_____

3. Was there anything that bothered you?

_____

_____

_____

_____

4. What did you learn about loving God?

_____

_____

_____

_____

5. What did you learn about loving others?

_____

_____

_____

_____

A Word About
The New International Reader's Version

Have You Ever Heard of the New International Version?

We call it the NIV. Many people read the NIV. In fact, more people read the NIV than any other English Bible. They like it because it's easy to read and understand.

And now we are happy to give you another Bible that's easy to read and understand. It's the New International Reader's Version. We call it the NIrV.

Who Will Enjoy Reading the New International Reader's Version?

People who are just starting to read will understand and enjoy the NIrV. Children will be able to read it and understand it. So will older people who are learning how to read. People who are reading the Bible for the first time will be able to enjoy reading the NIrV. So will people who have a hard time understanding what they read. And so will people who use English as their second language. We hope this Bible will be just right for you.

How Is the NIrV Different From the NIV?

The NIrV is based on the NIV. The NIV Committee on Bible Translation (CBT) didn't produce the NIrV. But a few of us who worked on the NIrV are members of CBT. We worked hard to make the NIrV possible. We used the words of the NIV when we could. When the words of the NIV were too long, we used shorter words. We tried to use words that are easy to understand. We also made the sentences of the NIV much shorter.

Why did we do all these things? Because we wanted to make the NIrV very easy to read and understand.

What Other Helps Does the NIrV Have?

We decided to give you a lot of other help too. For example, sometimes a verse is quoted from another place in the Bible. When it is, we tell you the Bible book, chapter and verse it comes from. We put that information right after the verse that quotes from another place.

We separated each chapter into shorter sections. We gave a title to almost every chapter. Sometimes we even gave a title to a section. We did these things to help you understand what the chapter or section is all about.

Another example of a helpful change has to do with the word "Selah" in the Psalms. What this Hebrew word means is still not clear. So, for now, this word is not helpful for readers. The NIV has moved the word to the bottom of the page. We have followed the NIV and removed this Hebrew word from the NIrV. Perhaps one day we will learn what this word means. But until then, the Psalms are easier to read and understand without it.

Sometimes the writers of the Bible used more than one name for the same person or place. For example, in the New Testament the Sea of Galilee is also called the Sea of Gennesaret. Sometimes it is also called the Sea of Tiberias. But in the NIrV we decided to call it the Sea of Galilee everywhere it appears. We called it that because that is its most familiar name.

We also wanted to help you learn the names of people and places in the Bible. So sometimes we provided names even in verses where those names don't actually appear. For example, sometimes the Bible says "the River" where it means "the Euphrates River." In those places, we used the full name "the Euphrates River." Sometimes the word "Pharaoh" in the Bible means "Pharaoh Hophra." In those places, we used his full name "Pharaoh Hophra." We did all these things in order to make the NIrV as clear as possible.

Does the NIrV Say What the First Writers of the Bible Said?

We wanted the NIrV to say just what the first writers of the Bible said. So we kept checking the Greek New Testament as we did our work. That's because the New Testament's first writers used Greek. We also kept checking the Hebrew Old Testament as we did our work. That's because the Old Testament's first writers used Hebrew.

We used the best copies of the Greek New Testament. We also used the best copies of the Hebrew Old Testament. Older English Bibles couldn't use those copies because they had not yet been found. The oldest copies are best because they are closer in time to the ones the first Bible writers wrote. That's why we kept checking the older copies instead of the newer ones.

Some newer copies of the Greek New Testament added several verses that the older ones don't have. Sometimes it's several verses in a row. This occurs at Mark 16:9 – 20 and John 7:53 — 8:11. We have included these verses in the NIrV. Sometimes the newer copies added only a single verse. An example is Mark 9:44. That verse is not in the oldest Greek New Testaments. So we put the verse number 43/44 right before Mark 9:43. You can look on the list below for Mark 9:44 and locate the verse that was added.

Verses That Were Not Found in Oldest Greek New Testaments

Matthew 17:21	But that kind does not go out except by prayer and fasting.
Matthew 18:11	The Son of Man came to save what was lost.
Matthew 23:14	How terrible for you, teachers of the law and Pharisees! You pretenders! You take over the houses of widows. You say long prayers to show off. So God will punish you much more.
Mark 7:16	Everyone who has ears to hear should listen.
Mark 9:44	In hell, / " 'the worms don't die, / and the fire doesn't go out.'
Mark 9:46	In hell, / " 'the worms don't die, / and the fire doesn't go out.'
Mark 11:26	But if you do not forgive, your Father who is in heaven will not forgive your sins either.
Mark 15:28	Scripture came true. It says, "And he was counted among those who disobey the law."
Luke 17:36	Two men will be in the field. One will be taken and the other left.
Luke 23:17	It was Pilate's duty to let one prisoner go free for them at the Feast.
John 5:4	From time to time an angel of the Lord would come down. The angel would stir up the waters. The first disabled person to go into the pool after it was stirred would be healed.
Acts 8:37	Philip said, "If you believe with all your heart, you can." The official answered, "I believe that Jesus Christ is the Son of God."
Acts 15:34	But Silas decided to remain there.
Acts 24:7	But Lysias, the commander, came. By using a lot of force, he took Paul from our hands.
Acts 28:29	After he said that, the Jews left. They were arguing strongly among themselves.
Romans 16:24	May the grace of our Lord Jesus Christ be with all of you. Amen.

What Is Our Prayer for You?

The Lord has blessed the New International Version in a wonderful way. He has used it to help millions of Bible readers. Many people have put their faith in Jesus after reading it. Many others have become stronger believers because they have read it.

We hope and pray that the New International Reader's Version will help you in the same way. If that happens, we will give God all the glory.

A Word About This Edition

This edition of the New International Reader's Version has been revised to include the changes of the New International Version. Over the years, many helpful changes have been made to the New International Version. Those changes were made because our understanding of the original writings is better. Those changes also include changes that have taken place in the English language. We wanted the New International Reader's Version to include those helpful changes as well. We wanted the New International Reader's Version to be as clear and correct as possible.

We want to thank the people who helped us prepare this new edition. They are Jeannine Brown from Bethel Seminary St. Paul, Yvonne Van Ee from Calvin College, Michael Williams from Calvin Theological Seminary, and Ron Youngblood from Bethel Seminary San Diego. We also want to thank the people at Biblica who encouraged and supported this work.

Kids, Read the Bible in a Whole New Way!

The Books of the Bible is a fresh way for kids to experience Scripture!
Perfect for reading together as a family or church group, this 4-part
Bible series removes chapter and verse numbers, headings, and special
formatting. Now the Bible is easier to read, and reveals the story of
God's great love for His people, as one narrative. Features the easy-to-
read text of the New International Reader's Version (NIrV). Ages 8-12.

Look for all four books in *The Books of the Bible*:

Covenant History
Discover the Beginnings of God's People   9780310761303

The Prophets
Listen to God's Messengers Tell about Hope and Truth   9780310761358

The Writings
Learn from Stories, Poetry, and Songs   9780310761334

New Testament
Read the Story of Jesus, His Church, and His Return   9780310761310

My Bible Story Coloring Book
The Books of the Bible   9780310761068

The Books of the Bible Children's Curriculum
9780310086161

These engaging lessons are formatted around
relatable Scripture references, memory verses, and
Bible themes. This curriculum has everything you
need for 32 complete lessons for preschool, early
elementary, and later elementary classes.

Read and Engage with Scripture in a Whole New Way!

The Books of the Bible is a fresh yet ancient presentation of Scripture ideal for personal or small group use. This 4-part Bible removes chapter and verse numbers, headings, and special formatting so the Bible is easier to read. The Bible text featured is the accurate, readable, and clear New International Version.

To get the entire Bible, look for all four books in *The Books of the Bible*:

Covenant History
Discover the Origins of God's People   9780310448037

The Prophets
Listen to God's Messengers Proclaiming Hope and Truth   9780310448044

The Writings
Find Wisdom in Stories, Poetry, and Songs   9780310448051

New Testament
Enter the Story of Jesus' Church and His Return   9780310448020

The Books of the Bible Study Journal   9780310086055

The Books of the Bible Video Study

9780310086109

Join pastor Jeff Manion and teacher John Walton as they look at the context and purpose for each book of the Bible. Included are (32) 10-minute sessions that can be used with large or small groups.